Navigating AI for Business

Uncertainty to Action

J. Ashley Woods, Sr.

Daniel J. Perrone

Published by

Intelligent Press

www.intelligentpress.co

INTELLIGENT
PRESS

Copyright & Legal Disclaimer

Published by Intelligent Press

www.intelligentpress.co

Library of Congress Control Number: 2025939977

ISBN: 979-8-218-69711

Printed in the United States of America

First Edition

Table of Contents

Introduction: Navigating this new era of AI for business.

Just a few years ago, artificial intelligence felt like something reserved for headlines, lab demos, or trillion-dollar tech companies. Today, it's in our inboxes, our phones, our social media posts, and increasingly—at the very center of how we run our businesses.

AI is no longer the future. It's the operating system of the present.

And with it comes both an extraordinary opportunity—and a leadership challenge.

This challenge is yours. Whether you're a business owner, entrepreneur, team leader, operator, or strategist—you are not just part of this era of AI for business. You own it.

This book is about helping you seize that opportunity with intention. It's here to show you how to adopt AI not as a gimmick, but with clarity, trust, and strategic purpose. Because the truth is, most businesses don't struggle with AI because they lack tools. They struggle because they haven't identified the right solutions, asked the right questions, discovered the right vision—or simply, because they don't know what action to take first.

You're not here to sign up for another platform.

You're here to build something that lasts.

Whether you lead a five-person firm, a fast-scaling team, or a mature mid-market operation, this book is your transition point—from uncertainty to action. From theory to traction. From observing AI to leading change.

Like you, we're entrepreneurs, business owners, and builders. We've come to understand what many still underestimate: AI is the Industrial Revolution, the Renaissance, and the Internet age rolled into one—but this time, it's exponential. It's not just reshaping business—it's redefining how teams are built, how customers are served, and how innovation flows through every department, every conversation, and every click.

And we're still in the earliest days.

AI is already the most powerful tool ever placed in the hands of the masses. And it belongs, not to tech giants or venture-backed labs, but to people like you and us—and the 80+ million businesses in the United States, and the hundreds of millions more around the world, who will define what AI becomes by how they choose to use it.

This book was written for you.

And like you, we've read hundreds of business books—and probably just as many on AI–and we've learned a lot about both along the way. We've also learned to keep the intro brief. You don't have time to waste—and frankly, in the time it takes to read twenty pages, AI will have already moved forward. If we do our job right, this book won't just keep up. It will give you the framework to lead AI transformation.

Because, you're not just entering the era of AI for business.

You're here to shape it.

This book is divided into five parts and twelve chapters—but more importantly, it follows a single, unshakable truth: people build businesses. AI helps us run them better.

We begin not with code or complexity, but with character—because leadership is at the heart of this transition.

The first part of the book lays the foundation. It explores the role of vision, values, and ethical responsibility in an age when machines are making decisions and software is scaling faster than strategy. Chapter 1 anchors us in timeless leadership principles—values, endurance, culture—that leadership is about who you choose to be and the actions you take. Chapter 2 builds on that by introducing the ethical considerations important to business leaders in the AI age. Drawing on global frameworks and leading thinkers, it helps to frame the important ethical discussion.

Once that foundation is in place, we move into understanding the landscape. Part II traces how we got here and what's driving AI's explosive growth—from its mathematical roots to the everyday tools already transforming business. Chapter 3 offers historical context, while Chapter 4 explores emerging AI solutions in sales, service, operations, and strategy. In Chapter 5, we zoom out—anticipating where this is all going. You'll discover how platforms, networks, and marketplaces are converging—and how to position your business to leverage the inflection point that has arrived. By the time you get to this place in the book, your understanding of what AI is and can do will be very sharp. We suspect you'll be making predictions about the future, just as we have.

With the terrain mapped, Part III helps you cut through the noise. We simplify. Chapter 6 filters the hype and narrows your focus to what actually drives value for business. Chapter 7 introduces one of the most important innovations of this AI era: modular, intelligent, and orchestrated AI Tasks. These are not theoretical abstractions. They are the foundation of the solution we have built, LIBBi, and the engine of the intelligent business.

The fourth part of the book brings the conversation back to people. Because while AI changes how work gets done, it's still us humans who carry the vision forward. Chapter 8 focuses on securing the future—emphasizing the role of data governance, transparency, and trust. Chapter 9 reframes work itself, shifting from execution to orchestration, and helping leaders prepare their teams for this new environment. Chapter 10 expands the idea of the workforce. It introduces new roles—Task Generalists and Specialists—and outlines how to develop and connect talent in a world where intelligent systems and human insight operate side by side.

At this point in the journey, we hope your mind is racing with the possibilities. We literally live in a time where we have the tools to mold the era of AI for business and you are artfully assembling the background, thought, and perspective to be a pioneer. And then, we build.

Part V turns the philosophy into practice. Chapter 11 gives you a complete, customizable playbook to implement what you've learned. With nine clear, actionable questions and a step-by-step planning guide, it helps you build your roadmap, identify gaps, and activate real transformation. Chapter 12 brings us full circle. It's a return to leadership—not as a recap, but as a re-centering. It reminds us that while technology may drive efficiency, it's people who build belief, shape culture, and lead teams through change. It's not enough to deploy AI. You have to lead through it—with empathy, conviction, and courage.

In the end, this book isn't just about understanding AI. It's about making the move to intelligent business—with clarity, with integrity, and with people at the center of every decision.

And that journey starts here—with you.

Why We Wrote This Book

We wrote this book because we needed it ourselves.

When we began building our company, InChannel AI, and launched what would become the first Intelligent Business Management Platform™, we weren't just developing a new kind of software—we were confronting, firsthand, the outdated systems, disconnected tools, and manual processes that still define how most businesses run. In building LIBBi, we made the move into AI—integrating intelligent Tasks into nearly every part of our operation. And through that journey, we didn't just deploy technology. We discovered the transformational power of AI for business.

This isn't a biography of our company, and it isn't a memoir. But woven through these chapters are the hard-won lessons, the tested insights, and the guidance we wish we'd had when we started. This book is shaped by what we've learned—through our own wins and failures, through the successes of companies we admire, and through the wisdom of the mentors and thought leaders who have inspired us along the way. We stand on the shoulders of many. We've drawn from their work and tried to assemble something that we hope helps accelerate your journey—faster, smoother, and with fewer wrong turns.

We also wrote this book because we've watched business owners wrestle with the unknowns of AI—not because they lack intelligence, but because they lack a map. We've seen smart leaders get overwhelmed by jargon, buried under buzzwords, and paralyzed by too many tools. Over and over again, we've heard the same quiet refrain:

"I know we need to do something with AI. I just have no idea where to start."

That's where this book comes in. This book isn't just about theory. It's about clarity. It's about connecting your values to your systems, your teams to your tools, and your vision to action. Its about naviigating AI for your business.

A very brief word about us—because this book isn't about us. It's about you.

We come from different professional backgrounds, but we share a common ethos: a passion for entrepreneurship, a deep intellectual curiosity, and a (sometimes irrational) drive to build what we believe will make the future better. One of us created and sold a tech company to Apple. The other led the evolution of one of the most storied national fundraising organizations in the country. We've both launched new ventures, scaled teams, and failed boldly at times. We've learned that technology is powerful—but every great movement is led by people. We're dreamers and builders. We believe that tomorrow can be better than today. And we believe in business as a force for good.

We also believe in proving our own ideas. That's why we became one of the first companies to operate using AI Tasks across nearly every business function—well before most people had even heard the term. And yes, we used AI to help write this book. Not to replace us, but to elevate us. It helped us research faster, phrase clearer, and organize more efficiently. But the ideas, the voice, the structure—those are ours. The AI was our tool, just like it can be yours.

That's the real promise of AI: not to replace human potential—but to accelerate it.

To you—the builders, the operators, the leaders of this new era—we offer this book with respect and conviction. You are the ones shaping the future, what we call *the era of AI for business*. This moment belongs to all of us: real people, solving real problems, running real businesses.

So let's lead with clarity. Let's build systems that reflect who we are. Let's scale not just technology—but trust, vision, and enduring businesses.

Let's make the move to intelligent business. Together.

And let's begin, as every great business does—with leadership.

The most powerful tool for navigating AI for business.

Ashley

Daniel

Part I: Leadership in the Age of AI

Chapter 1: The Timeless Core – Why Leadership Still Matters

Throughout every great transformation—whether steam-powered, silicon-driven, or cloud-enabled—one constant remains: leadership has always shaped what endures. The age of AI is no different. If anything, it raises the stakes. As intelligent systems begin to automate what we do, it's leadership that defines who we become. That's why we begin this book where every transformation should begin—not with tools, but with people. Not with platforms, but with principles. In a world increasingly powered by AI, we explore the kind of leadership that doesn't get replaced—but gets amplified.

Despite the excitement around AI's capabilities, no technology has ever led a company. People do. It is leadership—and more specifically, values-based leadership—that determines whether a business thrives or fails in uncertain times. Artificial intelligence is powerful, but it is only as purposeful, ethical, and effective as the humans who direct it.

There's a good chance you are building, leading, or preparing to launch something significant—perhaps even transformative. You may be pioneering within the new world of artificial intelligence or helping to shape what business and society will look like in the years ahead. Whether you're the founder of a startup, a leader inside a growing team, or someone crafting the very tools that will power the future, this chapter is for you.

While we acknowledge the vastness of the topic of leadership and the existing body of knowledge, our focus here is specific. We will concentrate on the timeless principles that define who a leader is and the essential actions that define what a leader does. Who am I and what do I do? The answers to these questions make a profound impact on your business, especially in the age of AI.

Timeless Principles in a Transforming World

We begin this discussion with values because they are the most important part of leadership. Everything else—vision, culture, creating enduring businesses and products—rests on this foundation. In fact, in our view it matters far less what a leader gets done than how they do it. And history has shown that what gets done is unlikely to endure unless it is rooted in values.

Values-based leadership prioritizes character and integrity, believing that these qualities ultimately drive positive outcomes. It's a commitment to principle over short-term performance gains. It's about acting with integrity, consistency, and a sense of duty to something greater than profit or position. In high-performing organizations, values are not decorative—they are functional. They inform decisions, shape culture, and earn trust.

Values-based leadership is deeply aligned with what scholars call transformational leadership—a style in which leaders inspire and elevate those they serve by appealing to higher ideals and moral values. Transformational leaders are change agents who empower others, align teams through a shared purpose, and model behaviors they hope to see.

While values-based leadership focuses on the internal compass of the leader—their integrity, ethics, and authenticity—transformational leadership adds the external outcome: mobilizing people toward a compelling future. Together, they form a holistic picture of leadership that is both principled and visionary.

In this book, we use this collective framework interchangeably and intentionally. Great leadership does not rely solely on operational excellence or technical know-how—it is anchored in purpose, guided by values, and expressed through transformation.

We all benefit from a rich library of leadership wisdom that has shaped our thinking on values-based leadership.

One of the leading authors and examples in this arena is Bill George, who is not just a theorist; he's a practitioner who put leadership principles into action during his tenure as CEO of Medtronic, the global medical technology company. Under his leadership from 1991 to 2001, Medtronic's market capitalization grew from $1.1 billion to over $60 billion, driven by a clear mission to "restore people to full life and health." George made values the cornerstone of decision-making, integrating purpose and ethics into every aspect of the business—from product development to patient care.

In his renowned book *Authentic Leadership* (and subsequent editions), George outlines five dimensions of values-based leadership:

- Purpose: Knowing what you stand for and aligning your actions with a meaningful mission.

- Values: Having a moral compass that guides decision-making, especially under pressure.

- Relationships: Building strong, genuine connections based on trust and transparency.

- Self-discipline: Staying focused, balanced, and resilient even when faced with distractions or challenges.

- Heart: Leading with compassion and empathy, understanding the human side of leadership.

George's philosophy is especially relevant in the age of AI. As businesses face increasing complexity and automation. *Authentic Leadership* reminds us that people don't follow strategies—they follow leaders. And leaders must be grounded in who they are and what they believe if they hope to inspire and sustain meaningful progress. While it may be true that today's AI can think, strategize, and set priorities and that tomorrow's AI will parallel and exceed human capabilities in many previously viewed executive-level functions, it cannot and will not replace the leadership dimensions of each of us.

The need for values-based leadership in times of transformation is not new. During the Industrial Revolution, when machines began replacing manual labor and traditional economic systems were upended, the world looked dramatically different than it had just a generation before. In this now historic period of disruption, new forms of leadership emerged—not just in business, but in labor, education, and governance.

George Cadbury, the British industrialist and co-founder of the Cadbury chocolate empire, was a great example of a transformational leader who demonstrated his values. He was not only known for transforming the cocoa industry but also for championing social reform during the height of the Industrial Revolution. Cadbury believed that business should serve humanity, and he put that belief into practice by embedding moral principles into every aspect of his company.

At a time when industrialization often meant low wages, long hours, and squalid living conditions, Cadbury pioneered a different model. In 1879, he moved the Cadbury factory from the polluted heart of Birmingham to a rural setting and founded Bournville—a purpose-built village designed to improve the lives of his workers. Bournville featured spacious housing with gardens, tree-lined streets, schools, medical services, and recreational facilities. It even included parks and a swimming pool, all rare for industrial laborers of that era.

This was not a public relations stunt. Cadbury believed that healthier, happier workers would be more productive and loyal, and that business could be a force for social good. Workers at Bournville had access to affordable housing with indoor plumbing, a revolutionary feature at the time. Children had access to quality education, and families had access to green space, fresh air, and cultural enrichment.

By contrast, many industrial workers of the period lived in crowded, unsafe tenement housing with no sanitation, no privacy, and limited access to clean water. Laborers elsewhere worked in unsafe factories under brutal conditions. Sickness, injury, and exploitation were widespread. Cadbury stood against this tide and used his influence to press for child labor laws and improvements in public health and welfare.

The impact was far-reaching. Bournville became a global model for humane industrial planning. Cadbury's approach influenced urban development, workplace reform, and the growing movement of corporate social responsibility. Perhaps most importantly, it showed that values-based leadership wasn't just morally superior—it was a competitive advantage. Cadbury's products gained trust. His workers stayed longer. His brand became synonymous with quality and compassion.

Cadbury exemplifies the kind of leadership that transformational eras demand: deeply rooted in values, boldly unafraid to challenge the status quo, and committed to people as the foundation of progress.

In a more recent era of transformation—the rise of the internet and digital globalization—another leader emerged who embodied values-based leadership: Paul Polman, former CEO of Unilever. Polman took the helm of the multinational consumer goods company in 2009, just as the world was reeling from the global financial crisis.

Rather than chase quarterly profits, Polman eliminated earnings guidance and focused on long-term sustainability. He launched the Unilever Sustainable Living Plan, committing the company to reduce its environmental footprint while increasing its social impact. This included ambitious goals like improving the health and well-being of over a billion people, sourcing 100% of agricultural raw materials sustainably, and enhancing livelihoods for millions of workers across the supply chain.

Critics questioned whether a publicly traded corporation could afford to prioritize ethics, environment, and fair treatment of its employees over short-term gains. But Polman held firm. He modeled the way with courage, enabling others to act by giving Unilever's global teams the authority and resources to innovate toward shared goals. He inspired a vision of capitalism that was not extractive, but expansive. The proverbial expansion of the pie.

The results? Unilever outperformed many of its peers, attracted mission-aligned talent, and built strong relationships with purpose-driven consumers. Investors began to reward companies for ethical practices. Polman not only changed Unilever—he helped shift expectations for what corporate leadership could be.

His legacy shows that even in a hyper-digital, profit-driven age, leadership rooted in values can still deliver competitive excellence, incredible shareholder value, and enduring good.

During our careers, we had the opportunity to work in organizations that held core values not as a plaque on the wall, but as the centerpiece of decision-making. We have, also, made our fair share of leadership mistakes. In our experiences, we saw firsthand the power of shared values to align teams, guide ethical choices, and inspire loyalty to the vision and business. When difficult decisions needed to be made—whether in restructuring, hiring, customer response, or innovation—leaders we followed returned again and again to those foundational principles. That clarity gave us courage, even in times of uncertainty.

One executive would often say, "when the path isn't clear, return to the values. They won't fail you." Another frequently shared the notion that "without a clear direction, any old road will do." Both proved true again and again, and now help form a compass for how we would lead our company InChannel AI. These experiences help to from a foundation of belief in what an enduring and values-centered business should be.

You may be familiar with James Kouzes and Barry Posner's *The Leadership Challenge*. Their research and framework further reinforces the teachings of Bill George and examples of Cadbury and Unilever. Their five practices—Model the Way, Inspire a Shared Vision, Challenge the Process, Enable Others to Act, and Encourage the Heart—are more than strategies; they are character-shaping habits rooted in both who a leader chooses to be and how a leader acts. One quote that continues to shape us: "Leaders go first. They set the example." Kouzes and Posner are exactly right.

These timeless truths also echo the teachings of faith-based leadership, where principles like servant leadership, stewardship, humility, and accountability create not just good business outcomes, but good societies. As echoed in scripture, "To whom much is given, much will be required"—a call to leadership that is responsible, thoughtful, and others-focused. While none of these ideas are unique to faith-based teachings, leaders grounded in faith traditions often see their role not as rulers of organizations but as caretakers of people, communities, and impact.

Not everyone goes to college, perhaps a discussion that could compose a book of its own, but we chose to do so and that time served as a catalyst for our leadership development. Even fewer choose to participate in Greek life, only about 10% by recent count (and actually increasing in recent years). In this microcosm, Fraternity life taught us many of the lessons we are discussing in this chapter in real-time through both success and failure. Parenthetically, fraternity culture is often misunderstood or unfairly caricatured. The reality for those who engage in it with intention and character is quite different. For us, and for many others, Fraternity was not about parties or prestige—it was about positive pressure, purpose, and personal growth.

It was, in many ways, a crucible. A place where young adults are thrust into situations that demand leadership without hierarchy, diplomacy among peers, and accountability to common ideals. It was here that we first encountered leadership not as a title, but as action—where being elected president or risk manager or philanthropy chair didn't mean power, it meant responsibility.

Fraternity or Greek life is one of the few spaces on a college campus where young leaders are handed meaningful responsibility and expected to make decisions that impact others. The environment is raw, peer-driven, and often unfiltered—exactly the kind of training ground that reveals your weaknesses and demands you confront them. It's not always graceful, but it is transformational.

In the absence of corporate structure and with minimal supervision, students in Greek life often govern themselves. They manage budgets, resolve conflict, plan large-scale events, enforce codes of conduct, and learn the cost of poor leadership in real time. While other campus organizations provide leadership opportunities, Greek life accelerates this experience because of its intensity and scale. It should not be skipped over that Greek life provides social development, also an important skill for leaders. The ability to connect with and help others take positive action is essential for every leader.

As members of the Sigma Chi Fraternity, we are guided by our core values that include courage, integrity, self-control, and fidelity. These values aren't just aspirational—they were expected during our days in college and beyond.

Importantly, these values are not unique to our Fraternity. You'll find them embedded in the creeds and cultures of other Greek organizations, social clubs, academic institutions, and professional environments. They are not the proprietary domain of Sigma Chi, nor are they exclusive to any group. That's the beauty and universality of values: when they are authentic, they transcend logos, organizations, and boundaries.

Courage, integrity, and fidelity are some of the qualities society looks for in leaders of any type. Whether you're in a boardroom, a locker room, a startup, or a service organization, these values can serve as a compass. What made our Fraternity experience powerful wasn't the uniqueness of the values—it was how deeply and consistently they were emphasized, expected, and tested.

They were not theoretical. They were lived, sometimes imperfectly, but always with an eye toward growth and accountability.

Another strong example of values at the center of leadership, and an inspiration, is the process by which the Navy selects SEAL Team Six members. When most people think of Navy SEAL Team Six, they imagine elite warriors with exceptional physical capabilities. And while physical strength and tactical skills are certainly required, they are not what sets SEAL Team Six apart. In fact, many candidates who meet the technical standards never make the cut. Why? Because what SEAL Team Six values most isn't performance under pressure—it's character under pressure.

In their selection process, candidates are evaluated not just on what they can do, but on how they behave when no one is watching. They are assessed for humility, composure, accountability, and—above all—trustworthiness. In one widely shared military leadership framework, SEALs use a two-axis matrix: performance on one axis, and trust on the other. And when forced to choose between a high-performer with low trust and a medium-performer with high trust, SEALs always choose trust. As one SEAL commander put it, *"We would rather have a guy who scores a 7 on performance and a 10 on trust than a guy who scores a 10 on performance and a 2 on trust."*

That's because high-performance in isolation is unstable. It can breed ego, chaos, and eventual collapse. But high trust creates resilience. It's what allows teams to operate in high-stakes environments, adapt to fluid conditions, and function without micromanagement—because everyone knows that the person next to them has their back. That trust, forged in silence, is what turns individuals into a team—and a team into a unit.

The same holds true in business. As we wrote earlier: *"People build businesses.*
AI helps us run them better." And people—especially in high-stakes, fast-
moving environments—don't want to follow the smartest person in the
room. They want to follow the most grounded. The person whose values
don't flicker under pressure. The leader who does what's right when no one
is watching.

SEAL Team Six doesn't just select for technical mastery. They select for
emotional discipline, cultural fit, and deeply embedded values. And in doing
so, they offer a powerful lesson to business leaders: when values are clear,
decisions are easy. And when character leads, trust follows.

As we conclude our focused discussion on values-based leadership, we
encourage you to ask yourself: what values are most important to me? Do I
actively apply these values to my leadership? Who you choose to be matters,
for your business and for those who make it happen.

Leaders Act as Architects of Vision, Culture, and Endurance

The leaders who create lasting outcomes aren't passive observers of
disruption—they are builders in the middle of it. They design with purpose,
act with conviction, and lay the groundwork for businesses that not only
survive but evolve. In an era defined by unrelenting change and exponential
innovation, this kind of leadership isn't a luxury. It's the line between drifting
with change—and defining it.

In the age of AI for business, leadership isn't about mastering every tool. It's
about architecting vision, culture, and endurance—and doing it deliberately.

As John C. Maxwell put it, *"A leader is one who knows the way, goes the way, and shows the way."* Leadership, in its most essential form, is the act of going first—with clarity, with courage, and with others in mind.

Because now, more than ever, leadership matters.

In the pursuit of speed, automation, and optimization, it's easy to forget what endures. But AI cannot replace character. Tools alone don't create trust. And automation doesn't replace judgment.

The more intelligent our systems become, the more vital it is that they're grounded in timeless principles—and that someone is responsible for making those principles real.

In moments of transformation—technological, social, organizational— leaders don't just react. They design. They build the frameworks their teams can live within: frameworks made of values, reinforced by vision, and held together by cultural integrity. They achieve enduring results. So now, we focus on creating vision, culture, and endurance, three of the most vital things that a leader does.

- Vision is the guiding force. It provides direction, meaning, and aspiration. It defines what success looks like and why the work matters.

- Culture is the atmosphere—the way people interact, behave, and belong. It determines what is expected, what is valued, and who fits.

- Endurance is the test of time. It ensures that the work is not fleeting, but built to last, to influence future generations, and to persist even as the world evolves.

When leaders invest in all three—when they discover, shape, and embed these elements—they lay a foundation that enables real and lasting transformation.

Finding and Codifying Vision

A leader often begins with an idea, a spark, or a rough outline of what could be. Rarely does the final vision arrive fully formed. More often, the complete vision emerges gradually—shaped by conversations, challenges, feedback, setbacks, and incremental achievements. It evolves and matures with experience and insight.

To "codify" a vision means taking this refined understanding and making it central, clear, and universally understood within the organization. It becomes the shared purpose—the guiding standard of alignment. Once a leader articulates the vision clearly, they can communicate it in ways that deeply resonate. It is not merely known but genuinely felt and embraced by every member of the team.

History provides numerous examples of leaders who refined and codified their visions over time. Consider, for instance, the story of Nelson Mandela. When Mandela first opposed apartheid in South Africa, he did not immediately possess a fully defined vision for a unified, equitable nation. His vision emerged and solidified through years of activism, dialogue, imprisonment, negotiation, and reconciliation. Mandela continually adjusted his approach in response to complex social dynamics, diverse perspectives, and evolving circumstances. Through all of this Mandela shaped a vision of a new South Africa defined by inclusivity, democracy, and justice. This vision was clearly articulated and ultimately guided an entire nation's transformation.

A more personal example is my dad (and this is Ashley writing for the moment). Though not recorded in history books, he embodied visionary leadership in tangible and practical ways. His life's work centered around Western North Carolina and East Tennessee, where he recognized potential in overlooked, neglected properties. Entirely self-taught, he intuitively transformed forgotten areas into meaningful places.

My dad saw possibilities instead of limitations. One notable example was a narrow, neglected parcel of land along a rural highway—little more than a runoff ditch. Where others saw inconvenience and minimal value, he envisioned a serene lake surrounded by woods, reflecting the beauty of nearby mountains. Over the course of several years, he patiently moved earth and meticulously shaped the landscape to align with his vision.

Ultimately, his consistent, focused effort turned a neglected ditch into a stunning, peaceful lake—a restorative retreat admired by all who experienced it. This was the essence of his leadership: quiet, consistent, and deeply rooted in a clear, evolving vision. Jim didn't impose his vision upon the world. Instead, he recognized it within the world and patiently brought it into being through deliberate and consistent action.

Both Mandela and my dad exemplify how great visions are discovered, refined, and codified. Leaders who achieve great results remain adaptable, open to new insights, and committed to clearly articulating their visions— allowing them to guide meaningful and enduring change.

Establishing the Framework of Culture

Once vision is clarified, leaders must establish the framework in which their people operate. This is culture—but not culture as a list of mottos or behavior codes. Culture is the invisible container that defines what is acceptable, what is rewarded, what is discouraged, and who thrives. It's how an organization answers the unspoken questions: *What are we here for? Who are we together? What are the non-negotiables?*

Leaders don't script every action. But they define the architecture. A strong cultural framework sets clear boundaries without micromanagement. It shapes decisions, guides behavior, and supports autonomy—not by dictating actions, but by clarifying purpose. When done right, culture becomes the quiet voice in the room when the leader isn't there.

And yet, as obvious as this may sound to seasoned business operators, we'll say what many are already thinking: *creating culture is not easy.* Perhaps more obvious still—*no two business cultures are the same.* What works in a fast-scaling tech startup might fail in a precision-driven law firm. The core values might be consistent, but the expression of those values must be authentic to the business and its people.

At InChannel AI, we've worked to create a culture that reflects the leaders we choose to be. It's built around high performance, ethical boundaries, innovation, and humility. We offer a description of our culture not as a prescription, but as a single real-world example:

- Attitude is everything. Positivity, resilience, and emotional intelligence create cohesion and momentum. People with a constructive, humble mindset fuel collaboration.

- Do what it takes—with integrity. High-performing cultures embrace grit, but never at the expense of values. Doing what it takes means effort, ownership, and sacrifice—but always within ethical bounds.

- Hard work is a given. In a culture of trust, no one has to be reminded to work hard. Effort is expected and respected.

- Customer is our focus. We don't just serve customers—we obsess over them. The voice of the customer is present in every meeting, every decision, and every roadmap.

- Hyper intellectual curiosity wins. Great cultures are powered by people who ask "why?" and "what if?"—people who challenge assumptions and seek better ways.

You can see this mindset embodied in the way Elon Musk approached the early days of SpaceX. As Walter Isaacson recounts in his biography, aptly titled *Elon Musk,* Musk didn't just lead from the top—he embedded himself in the trenches. He read rocket engineering textbooks, interrogated suppliers, and challenged every assumption. The result? The Merlin engine—a radically simplified, highly efficient propulsion system with fewer moving parts than any comparable model at the time. It wasn't built on luck. It was built on curiosity, persistence, and a cultural refusal to accept the status quo.

This kind of culture—a culture of learning, problem-solving, and intellectual audacity—becomes the foundation for both resilience and reinvention.

But culture is not just an internal blueprint—it's also shaped by context. One of the great myths in business is that leadership looks the same everywhere. That a great leader in one company, in one country, or in one role will automatically be a great leader in another. But the truth is more nuanced. This gets a bit more complicated when working to architect business culture in a different human culture.

As one of our mentors and a giant in the business world, Robert D. "Bob" Johnson writes in *Global Business Leadership*:

> "Leaders must understand not only their own strengths, but how those strengths are perceived by others. What inspires trust in one culture may signal arrogance in another. What feels transparent in one environment may feel overly exposed in another."

This doesn't mean leaders need to become chameleons or abandon their values. It means they must be culturally intelligent, both to the culture of the business and to the culture where it operates. The most effective leaders understand the difference between principle and expression. They don't compromise what they believe—but they do tailor how they communicate, motivate, and guide. They architect a winning business culture that is sensitive to the surrounding human culture.

This becomes even more essential in the context of AI. As automation scales and digital tools become more embedded in everyday operations, leaders must ensure that what gets scaled aligns with the people and cultures it's meant to serve. AI can distribute decisions, automate approvals, and streamline interactions. But it's leadership—and leadership alone—that keeps the human element intact.

A great example to bring all of this together is the leadership path of Herb Kelleher, the legendary co-founder and longtime CEO of Southwest Airlines. Kelleher didn't build an airline. He built a culture—one that prioritized people, joy, trust, and accountability. His mantra was simple: *"If you treat your employees right, they'll treat your customers right. And if you treat your customers right, your shareholders will be happy."*

That ethos powered Southwest through recessions, deregulation, mergers, and industry disruption. Not because they had the best planes or the most routes—but because they had a cultural architecture that outlasted any one leader.

That's what great leadership does. It builds frameworks that endure.

So as you define your own business culture—whether you're leading five people or five hundred and whether your leading in Sarasota, Islamabad, or Rome—ask yourself not just what you want your values to be, but how you want them to be experienced, expressed, and sustained. Because culture isn't a plaque on the wall. It's the architecture that shapes behavior when no one's watching.

And in an era where AI will scale whatever system you give it, your culture isn't just internal code—it's the foundation of everything to come.

Creating an Enduring Business or Product

While it does not end the list of actions that leaders take, we conclude with the effort that leaders make to create an enduring business or product. Enduring leaders instil permanence in the work, making sure that what is built lasts beyond them. Endurance doesn't mean permanence in every task, but rather continuity of vision, of values, and of impact.

One striking metaphor is Jeff Bezos' 10,000 Year Clock, a project unlike anything else being built today. Located deep within a mountain in West Texas, the clock is designed to tick once every year, with a chime once every thousand years. Its intended lifespan? Ten thousand years.

This isn't just an engineering marvel—it's a philosophical monument. Bezos and the team behind the Long Now Foundation designed the clock to challenge our perception of time, to force us to think not in quarterly earnings, election cycles, or product launches, but in civilizational terms. The clock is mechanical, powered by thermal cycles and solar alignment. It is built to endure—through storms, wars, climate change, and perhaps even the rise and fall of modern civilization.

The gears and components are made of materials like titanium and ceramic, chosen for their durability across millennia. Everything is designed to be understandable by future generations—even if language or technology evolves beyond recognition. The mechanisms rely on natural cycles like sunlight and gravity rather than electronic systems that may not exist in the distant future.

Building something to last 10,000 years demands a mindset entirely foreign to most modern endeavors. It requires foresight, discipline, and reverence for continuity. It's not just about durability—it's about *intent*.

Bezos has said that part of the clock's meaning is about encouraging long-term responsibility. In a world obsessed with the now, the 10,000 Year Clock is a whisper from the future, reminding us that legacy is built one enduring choice at a time. It's meant to tick once a year, chime once a millennium, and run for ten thousand years. This project poses a quiet question to every business and leader: what are you building that someone even thirty years from now will recognize, use, or be inspired by?

Consider also the Egyptian pyramids. Built over 4,500 years ago, they were not only architectural feats, but cultural symbols of identity and civilization. The leaders behind these projects weren't thinking in quarterly increments.

Another powerful example of endurance comes from the more modern hospitality industry. J. Willard Marriott, Sr.—founder of the Marriott Corporation—built more than a hotel brand; he established a legacy of service and people-first leadership that continues to shape global hospitality decades later. Born the son of a sheep rancher in Utah, Marriott started with a root beer stand in Washington, D.C., in 1927. What set him apart wasn't just business savvy, but a relentless focus on taking care of people.

His mantra was simple: "Take care of your people and they'll take care of your customers, and the customers will come back." That philosophy wasn't marketing—it was a way of life. Marriott personally visited hotels, talked to housekeepers, listened to bellhops, and never let size or scale become an excuse to lose touch. He believed in getting the small things right, in part because he knew they were what made people feel valued.

When Bill Marriott Jr. took over the company, he built on that legacy. The leadership philosophy endured across generations. Today, Marriott is the largest hotel company in the world, but what continues to differentiate it is its deep-rooted culture of service, trust, and operational excellence.

In business, endurance means creating systems, habits, and principles that don't expire with market trends or leadership turnover. It's about legacy. And leaders who commit to endurance create organizations that outlast crises, fads, and even their own tenure. And just because AI is moving fast and we are all working in a rapidly evolving environment doesn't mean that our efforts cannot be enduring. In fact, perhaps more than ever before that's exactly what we should endeavor to achieve.

Case studies: What can we learn from others' successes and failures

Apple: Values and Vision

Apple offers one of the most iconic examples of leadership-driven success, pulling together both the elements of who we choose to be as leaders and the actions we take. When Steve Jobs returned to Apple in 1997, the company was struggling with declining innovation and eroded brand identity. His leadership transformed Apple not simply through design or product decisions, but through a reassertion of clarity, vision, and culture.

Jobs modeled the principle of "Inspire a Shared Vision," from the teachings of Kouzes and Posner earlier discussed. This aligned the company around a mission to create beautifully intuitive technology. His leadership was not flawless, but it was resolute. Apple became synonymous with innovation and excellence because leadership set that expectation from the top.

After Jobs, Tim Cook demonstrated a different kind of leadership. Grounded in operational excellence and empathy, Cook proved that quiet leadership can also sustain greatness. Under his stewardship, Apple grew to become the world's most valuable company—proof that leadership is not one-size-fits-all, but it must be principled.

Enron: The Collapse of Integrity

Enron's story is one of visionary thinking corrupted by the absence of ethical leadership. Initially seen as a trailblazer in energy trading, Enron built complex financial instruments that were used to hide debt and inflate profits. It was a culture that modeled the opposite of Kouzes and Posner's five practices: leaders didn't "Model the Way"—they manipulated it. They inspired visions rooted in illusion. They enabled wrongdoing and discouraged transparency.

Ken Lay and Jeffrey Skilling surrounded themselves with yes-men. There was no fidelity to truth or responsibility. Eventually, the façade collapsed, destroying the lives of employees and wiping out retirement savings. Enron remains one of the most devastating leadership failures in American corporate history.

Circuit City: Lose the Culture and Lose the Company

Circuit City was once a dominant electronics retailer, even outpacing Best Buy in the 1990s. But a series of short-sighted leadership decisions eroded the company from the inside.

In 2007, the board chose to lay off its most experienced salespeople to save money. This destroyed employee morale and crippled customer experience. The leadership failed to "Enable Others to Act" and "Encourage the Heart." These decisions broke trust internally and externally, and the company filed for bankruptcy just two years later.

Best Buy, by contrast, invested in its people and empowered store leaders. It remains a strong retailer in an Amazon-dominated world. The difference? Leadership that valued culture and people.

Connecting the Dots: Our Path to LIBBi

When our team at InChannel AI began exploring artificial intelligence—first individually as entrepreneurs going back almost a decade and later as a unified company—we recognized that we were entering an arena filled with excitement, confusion, and fragmented solutions. Rather than chasing short-term trends or quick successes, we committed ourselves to something bigger and more enduring: creating the world's first Intelligent Business Management Platform™. Our goal wasn't simply to add AI to existing business processes; it was to fundamentally redefine how businesses operate in this new, AI-driven era.

Our vision was ambitious yet clear: to build a transformational system that would enable businesses of all sizes to harness AI safely, effectively, and meaningfully. AI that *worked* for everyone. We weren't interested in developing just another productivity tool. Instead, we aimed to revolutionize the way work gets accomplished, providing a platform that was genuinely intelligent, deeply intuitive, and refreshingly simple.

However, this vision didn't come fully formed from day one. Like most meaningful innovations, it emerged gradually. We started with a mix of ideas, shared aspirations, and yes, even some disagreement. But through deep exploration, continuous dialogue, practical experimentation, and extensive feedback, our vision became clearer, stronger, and fully aligned.

Once we articulated and codified this vision, we knew our next step was to create the right culture—one that would nurture, support, and sustain our ambitions. We intentionally built this culture around key principles that reflected our values and goals.

From the outset, our aim was clear: we didn't want our product to become just another passing trend in AI technology. Instead, we sought to establish an enduring platform and company that would evolve with the times and serve as a stable foundation for businesses navigating the future.

Along the way, we made plenty of mistakes and encountered numerous challenges—and we fully expect more ahead. Yet, our approach of grounding ourselves in values-based leadership, clearly defining our vision, intentionally shaping our culture, and striving for lasting impact has proven effective. Time will be the test of the endurance of our company and product, but, the point here is our intention–to build something with an enduring impact. And, it is a point, too, that we hope you endeavor to build into your business and, perhaps, the next 10,000 year clock.

Final Thoughts: AI Needs Human Leadership

Throughout this chapter, we've explored leadership not just as a function of strategy, but as a reflection of enduring values. The principles of courage, integrity, self-control, and fidelity are not exclusive to any one organization and are merely an example of timeless values. Core values help to form a foundation of trust, the scaffolding of good judgment, and the compass for responsible progress. Whether taught in Fraternities, families, military academies, or community centers, core values shape the kind of leaders the world needs most—especially in moments of transformation.

In an era defined by technological acceleration, it's tempting to believe that new tools will solve old problems, and they often can. But tools do not lead—people do. And the kind of people who will successfully lead us through the AI era are those grounded in something deeper than algorithms or margins. They are grounded in values.

As we enter the era of AI for business, the need for principled leadership doesn't fade—it becomes more urgent. AI will scale whatever we design— our priorities, our decisions, our ethics.

In the AI age, speed will be seductive. Automation will be easy. But wisdom will be rare.

True leadership is not reactive. It's proactive, principled, and people-centered. Whether you're a startup founder or a Fortune 100 CEO, the challenge is the same: what kind of leaders we choose to be? What actions will you take?

Chapter 2: The Ethical Compass – Ethics and Guardrails for the Era of AI for Business

Creating Ethical Guardrails for AI

In Chapter 1, we explored how values shape leadership—and how leadership, in turn, shapes culture. As it turns out, the same principle applies to the systems we build. Just as an organization's culture creates the boundaries for human behavior, the rise of artificial intelligence and machine learning demands its own framework: ethical guardrails that reflect not just what a system can do, but what it *should* do.

These guardrails aren't checklists. They're not lines of code. They are reflections of our core values—applied with intentionality and scaled through technology. And it's no coincidence that this conversation lives in the section of this book about leadership. Because it's leaders—*you*—who decide how those values show up in practice.

As AI becomes more embedded in the decisions that shape our daily lives, the questions it raises are no longer hypothetical. Who gets hired? Who gets approved? What news gets seen? How is personal data used—or misused? In each case, AI isn't just calculating—it's influencing human experience. And that kind of power demands responsibility.

We're not here to offer final answers. But we do hope to raise the right questions. Because whether you're building products, teams, or entire companies, you are also building the moral compass of the systems you deploy. That's not a side task. That's leadership.

And like every meaningful act of leadership, ethics isn't something you check off. It's something you choose.

The Need for Ethical Guardrails

Eric Schmidt, in *The Age of AI: And Our Human Future*, argues that we are entering an era where AI will not just support decision-making but shape society itself. "The first question of AI governance is not what can it do, but what should it do," he writes. Schmidt and his co-authors raise urgent concerns: Will AI undermine democratic discourse? Will it accelerate inequality? Who controls these systems, and who is accountable when they fail?

The book suggests that AI systems must be treated as critical infrastructure—demanding the same level of foresight, oversight, and global cooperation as nuclear or biotech innovations.

Key paraphrased questions posed include:

- What happens when AI systems act unpredictably?

- How do we preserve human agency in an automated world?

- What governance models are best suited for transnational AI platforms?

These questions require answers, the attainment of which will require broad discussion and debate from sources across all industries and fields of expertise. Schmidt's work further adds urgency to the need for ethics in design—not after AI causes harm, but before it does. His message echoes Chapter 1's call: just as leaders shape culture before crisis hits, so too must we embed ethics before AI becomes irreversibly embedded in our lives.

Perhaps the best way to frame the discussion, and equip you with the framework to reach your own decisions about ethical considerations in AI, is to explore what various scholars have argued. Let's consider several of the leading thinkers in this arena.

From Harm Avoidance to Moral Reasoning

Wendell Wallach and Colin Allen's *Moral Machines* tackles one of the most provocative questions in the field: Can machines be taught to make ethical decisions? Their answer is layered and nuanced. They propose that artificial moral agents should be developed on a spectrum—from systems that avoid harm by design (implicit ethical agents) to those capable of engaging in actual moral reasoning (explicit ethical agents).

This work presents a true philosophical stance: ethics is a capability that must be intentionally embedded into machines, not assumed. The authors explore practical strategies like constraint satisfaction, value-sensitive design, and machine learning models that can evolve with ethical feedback.

Key Takeaways:

- Ethical AI systems must be both rule-based and adaptive.

- Designers must think like ethicists, not just engineers.

- The future of AI depends on embedding moral reasoning into machine design.

Moral Machines influenced early thinking in AI policy circles and laid the foundation for current conversations about alignment, interpretability, and algorithmic responsibility.

The Relational Ethics of AI

Mark Coeckelbergh's *AI Ethics* presents one of the most philosophically rich perspectives in the modern ethics discourse. Rather than framing ethics as a list of rules or checklists, Coeckelbergh invites readers to think deeply about the meaning, relationships, and societal impacts that AI creates. He calls for an approach to AI ethics that is less about compliance and more about engaged interpretation—a form of moral responsibility that adapts to context, complexity, and change.

One of his most significant contributions is what he calls the "relational turn" in ethics. Rather than asking, "Is this algorithm fair?" Coeckelbergh encourages us to ask, "How does this AI system affect relationships—between people, between people and machines, and across social institutions?" In this sense, ethics is not just about logic or legality. It's about the lived experience of technology users.

He also critiques the myth of technological neutrality. Code, design decisions, and data all carry embedded values—whether conscious or not. Thus, developers are not just building tools; they are shaping social reality.

"The ethics of AI is not merely about good programming. It is about what kind of world we are building," Coeckelbergh emphasises.

He further argues for a hermeneutic approach—one where ethics is an interpretive act requiring continuous reflection, dialogue, and stakeholder participation.

In practice, this means:

- Involving users in the design process (participatory ethics)

- Anticipating long-term impacts through scenario modeling

- Embedding ethics in every stage of the AI lifecycle—not just post-deployment

- Encouraging developers and business leaders to think of themselves as moral agents, not just engineers or executives

In our view, Coeckelbergh's work emphasizes the need for input from many, including those of us who lead, operate, and are building businesses.

Operationalizing Data Values in Business
Kord Davis' *Business Data Ethics* is a practical guide that bridges the gap between abstract ethical principles and the day-to-day decisions businesses make about data. He argues that ethical behavior with data is not just a matter of legal compliance or technical configuration—it's a leadership imperative that must be embedded into company culture. Davis frames data ethics as a business challenge that touches strategy, brand reputation, product design, marketing, and organizational trust.

At the core of his argument is this: businesses must first define their values before they can act ethically with data. Without a shared understanding of what a company believes is "right," employees default to personal judgment, which can be inconsistent or misaligned with organizational goals. Davis proposes a "data values" framework, which helps organizations explicitly articulate principles that guide how data is collected, interpreted, shared, and monetized.

He outlines a multi-part process for embedding ethics into business operations:

- Clarify Core Values: Start with a shared understanding of your organization's principles, such as respect, transparency, or user empowerment.

- Operationalize Those Values: Translate them into specific policies, such as limits on behavioral tracking or opt-in data practices.

- Engage in Dialogue: Foster open discussion across departments to ensure values are understood and reflected in product decisions.

- Support with Governance: Implement cross-functional ethical review processes that include product, legal, design, and data science teams.

"Ethics doesn't live in the technology. It lives in the people who make decisions about the technology," Davis writes.

He also reminds readers that ethical choices are rarely black and white. Instead, they live in grey zones where trade-offs must be navigated—between personalization and privacy, speed and transparency, or growth and fairness. Davis offers decision-making models to help navigate these tensions, urging leaders to be proactive rather than reactive.

To bring this discussion closer to home, we consider our own customers using our LIBBi solution. In building our product we faced the question at the core of Davis' work: if data is your most powerful asset, then you must have ethical clarity about how you use it.

It may be worth asking yourself as a business leader: Am I comfortable feeding my critical business data into AI? We'll come back to this question later in the book.

As we conclude our limited review of what scholars say on this topic, and we encourage you to do broader research if this discussion has peeked your curiosity, let us emphasize that establishing ethical guardrails is not just a regulatory checkbox or a crisis response mechanism—it is a foundational act of leadership. Just as a strong organizational culture defines what behavior is acceptable within a company, ethical frameworks shape how AI behaves within society. These frameworks—whether proposed by governments, tech leaders like Eric Schmidt, or philosophers like Mark Coeckelbergh—underscore a shared understanding: AI is not neutral, and its trajectory is not predetermined. It reflects the values we embed, the questions we ask, and the boundaries we draw. If we want AI to amplify human potential rather than diminish it, we must ensure our innovations are guided by principles as ambitious as our technologies. Ethics, in this light, becomes not a brake on progress but the steering wheel that keeps us on course.

Clearly, much thought is being given to ethical guardrails for Artificial Intelligence and Machine Learning, but what are governments doing in this regard? Let's explore the many regulatory schemes that have been adopted or are in discussion throughout our world.

Global Frameworks for Ethical AI

Governments and international organizations around the world have recognized the need to establish robust ethical frameworks to guide the development and deployment of artificial intelligence. While their approaches vary, each reflects a growing consensus that AI must be aligned with human rights, public trust, and sustainable progress. Lets dig into the most prominent structures shaping the global AI landscape today.

European Union's AI Act (2021)

The EU AI Act is the first comprehensive legal framework for AI regulation globally. It adopts a risk-based classification system that categorizes AI applications into four levels—unacceptable, high, limited, and minimal risk. Applications deemed "unacceptable," such as social scoring or real-time biometric surveillance in public spaces, are banned outright. High-risk systems—like those used in hiring, education, or credit scoring—must meet strict transparency, accountability, and documentation requirements. The Act mandates human oversight, accuracy standards, and clear data governance. Its primary objective is to ensure AI technologies do not undermine fundamental rights, while still encouraging innovation across the EU.

OECD AI Principles (2019)

Adopted by over 40 countries, the Organization for Economic Cooperation and Development (OECD) AI Principles sets out five values-based principles to foster trust in AI systems. These include: (1) inclusive growth and sustainable development, (2) human-centered values and fairness, (3) transparency and explainability, (4) robustness and security, and (5) accountability. The OECD also encourages governments to establish policy and regulatory frameworks that promote innovation while ensuring public trust. This framework has been influential in shaping national strategies, particularly for countries lacking detailed regulatory approaches of their own.

UNESCO's Recommendation on the Ethics of Artificial Intelligence (2021)

UNESCO's framework is one of the most globally inclusive efforts to define AI ethics, with over 190 member states contributing. It focuses on ensuring that AI contributes to peace, human dignity, and inclusive societies. Its guiding pillars include environmental sustainability, cultural diversity, fairness, and data governance. The recommendation emphasizes the importance of impact assessments, ethical education, and fostering diversity in AI development. Unlike many Western frameworks, it highlights the intersection between technology and broader social justice concerns, especially in the Global South.

The National Institute of Standards and Technology (NIST) in the United States developed its AI Risk Management Framework (AI RMF) to help organizations design trustworthy AI systems. Rather than prescribing specific technical standards, the AI RMF encourages a flexible, voluntary, and outcomes-focused approach tailored to sector-specific risks. The framework identifies key characteristics of trustworthy AI, including validity, reliability, robustness, privacy, fairness, accountability, and transparency. It promotes an iterative lifecycle approach—Plan, Map, Measure, and Manage—and provides a toolkit to assess and mitigate risk throughout development and deployment. It is rapidly becoming a cornerstone for responsible AI practices in U.S. industry and government.

Common Themes Across Frameworks

While each framework has unique emphasis areas, several common themes consistently emerge:

- **Human Oversight and Agency:** AI systems should augment, not replace, human decision-making. Clear accountability pathways and fail-safes are essential.

- **Fairness and Non-Discrimination:** Systems must be tested for bias, particularly those deployed in socially sensitive domains like hiring, lending, or law enforcement.

- **Transparency and Explainability:** Users and regulators must be able to understand how and why decisions are made by AI.

- Accountability and Governance: There must be traceable documentation of AI system design, performance, and ethical considerations.

- Safety and Robustness: Systems must be resilient to manipulation, attack, or failure—and undergo ongoing monitoring and validation.

These themes are not merely technical best practices. They represent a shared ethical consensus on how to responsibly steer AI innovation. They remind us that AI does not exist in a vacuum. It reflects and reinforces the values we choose to embed—and the consequences of ignoring that responsibility are too great to risk.

Connecting the Dots: A Case Study in Building an Ethics Roadmap

We said at the outset that this book is not about our company, and we will honor that commitment. But, we may use our company as a case study and example at times, and here is our first opportunity to share what we have learned as an intended helpful example. At InChannel AI, we worked to treat ethics not as an afterthought, but as an operating principle. As we built our LIBBi—the world's first Intelligent Business Management Platform™—we looked to the best of what the world's scholars, governments, and technologists were doing to establish ethical standards for AI. We reviewed frameworks like the EU's AI Act, NIST's AI Risk Management Framework, UNESCO's global recommendations, and the thought leadership of philosophers like Mark Coeckelbergh and Kord Davis. These models didn't just influence us—they helped shape the core design of our platform. We found these perspectives to be a tremendous asset in an arena of AI where many questions and unresolved debates still exist, as you now understand.

We ended up taking as straightforward an approach as we could conceive: adopt the strongest global principles, tailor them for practical use, and raise the bar where necessary.

With this as our guide, we worked to incorporate safeguards, transparency, and agency into every layer of the user experience:

- Explainability by Design: Every AI Task, functionality that uses AI to take business action, includes built-in transparency mechanisms so users understand what the AI is doing, why it's doing it, and how it arrived at its conclusions. We do not hide behind black boxes.

- Bias Detection and Fairness Retesting: We regularly test our models for bias using real-world simulations and diverse data. When disparities are found, models are re-trained to ensure fairness across sectors, company sizes, and user types.

- Human-in-the-Loop Decision Making: For any Task that supports consequential or high-stakes decisions—such as hiring, budgeting, or legal processing—LIBBi ensures that final control always rests with a human user. Our AI doesn't replace judgment; it supports it.

- Continuous Ethical Oversight: We conduct recurring internal ethics reviews for every major product update and consult with external advisors when dealing with novel or sensitive use cases. Our ethics process is not static—it is iterative and evolving.

We also believe data belongs to the businesses that generate it—full stop. So as we built our solution, we made sure that data is not shared, is not sold,

and is never used to train broader large language models (LLMs) outside the user's explicit permission.

Here's what that means in practice:

- Siloed Data Architecture: Every business's data is securely siloed and compartmentalized. Even within LIBBi, each business operates in its own walled environment, protected by layered encryption and access controls.

- Zero Cross-Training Policy: No data inputted by a business is used to train or improve other AI models on our platform or externally. This ensures both privacy and competitive protection.

- Single-Source Access for the Business: While we protect and silo data, we also empower businesses to use it seamlessly across all of their AI Tasks. LIBBi's centralized data hub allows every Task to draw from the same structured, verified source of truth—reducing duplication, increasing accuracy, and accelerating task performance.

- Full Transparency and Control: Businesses always know what data is being used, where it lives, and how it flows across Tasks. Consent, visibility, and auditability are built into every interaction.

To close out this case study, we also found opportunities to adopt principles found in many of the global frameworks we discussed earlier in this chapter:

- From Europe's AI Act: We adopt a risk-based approach to system transparency and governance.

- From NIST's framework: We operationalize trust through internal risk controls and lifecycle management.

- From UNESCO and OECD: We emphasize human agency, sustainability, and inclusive innovation.

But beyond that, we return to our own values—courage, integrity, self-control, and fidelity. These guide not only how LIBBi behaves, but how we as a company build, govern, and evolve.

We believe this ethical framework is right for our solution. If we do this right, it will also continue to evolve as we all learn more and benefit from feedback and broader debate. But, importantly, our framework may not be the right one for all AI solutions or businesses. But, we hope that you are not equipped with enough of the key questions, considerations, and views to build your own position on how ethics should be treated and intentionally designed into your intelligent business.

Final Thoughts: Design with Values, Deploy with Integrity
AI will become more powerful, more predictive, and more embedded in our lives. The question is not whether we will use it—but how. The best AI systems don't just perform well. They align with who we are.

Just as Chapter 1 reminded us that leadership is rooted in courage, integrity, and fidelity, Chapter 2 urges us to bring those same virtues to our AI decisions. Ethics is not a constraint. It is a compass.

In the era of AI, speed will be seductive, and automation will be easy. But wisdom? Wisdom will be rare.
Design with values. Deploy with integrity. Let ethics be both your competitive advantage—and your enduring legacy.

AI will become more powerful, more predictive, and more embedded in our lives. The question is not whether we will use it—but how. The best AI systems don't just perform well. They align with who we are.

Just as Chapter 1 reminded us that leadership is rooted in courage, integrity, and fidelity, Chapter 2 urges us to bring those same virtues to our AI decisions. Ethics is not a constraint. It is a compass—a guide that helps us move with intention and foresight.

As you move forward in your journey—whether you're developing AI, deploying it in business, or shaping policy—consider the following:

- Are your AI systems reinforcing your organization's values, or are they eroding them?

- Have you built in mechanisms for transparency, fairness, and accountability?

- Are your data practices clear, consent-driven, and respectful of users' rights?

How would your stakeholders—employees, customers, communities—describe the ethics of your AI decisions?

Are you treating ethics as a checklist, or as a living, breathing part of your innovation culture?

If your AI system were to fail publicly, would your organization be proud of the process that created it?

Ethics, as explored in this chapter, is not a separate consideration—it is part of a broader system of values-based leadership introduced in Chapter 1. As we continue forward in this book, remember that ethics is not a side constraint—it is part of the leadership system you are building to ensure trust, alignment, and resilience in an AI-powered business environment.

The age of AI demands not just brilliance, but wisdom. Not just speed, but reflection. The organizations that thrive in this new era will not be those who move the fastest, but those who move with the most clarity of purpose.

Design with values. Deploy with integrity. Let ethics be your competitive advantage—and your legacy.

Chapter 3: The Path to Now – A Brief History of AI

In Chapter 2, we explored the ethical foundations that must guide how we build and deploy AI—foundations that begin, as all enduring systems do, with leadership and values. But to lead well, we must also understand what we're leading through. That's where we turn now: not to the future, but to the path that brought us here.

This chapter shifts focus. Until now, we've assumed a certain level of experience—tenured leaders, seasoned operators, people who've navigated disruption before. But here, we hit reset. Because when it comes to AI—its history, its classifications, its current capabilities—the playing field is far more level than it seems. If you're new to the space, you're not behind. And if you've been watching closely, you know the terrain still shifts beneath our feet.

We remember a conversation from the early days of building LIBBi. We were spitballing ideas for a voice-enabled interface—imagine if a business operator on the go could speak a command, and the system would respond. At the time, it felt futuristic. Ambitious. Maybe two or three years away. We were wrong. Within a month, LIBBi could talk.

It wasn't perfect—misplaced punctuation, missing words—but it was speaking. That moment revealed something essential about the nature of AI: it evolves in sudden leaps and lingering delays. Some capabilities feel years out—until they're here. Others remain oddly unsolved, untouched by decades of advancement. For business leaders, this is part of the reality: we're working with a system that is both dazzlingly fast and maddeningly unfinished. And that's okay.

No one knows everything about AI—not even those who build it. The key isn't to master it all. It's to understand where it came from, what it's capable of today, and how it might shape what comes next.

In this chapter, we'll walk that path together. Our goal is to:

- Provide historical context to the emergence of modern AI

- Define foundational concepts like LLMs, generative AI, agents, and wrappers

- Explain what today's AI systems can actually do—and what they can't

- And introduce a new model for applying AI to business: the Intelligent Business Management Platform™

Whether you're new to the space or already knee-deep in experimentation, this chapter is designed to meet you where you are—and give you the context to move forward, with clarity and confidence.

The Evolution of AI: From Theory to Transformation

To understand today's landscape, we must first understand how AI began. While "artificial intelligence" as a term was first coined in 1956 at the Dartmouth Summer Research Project on Artificial Intelligence, the field's roots run much deeper—into the realms of mathematics, computer science, neuroscience, and philosophy. And, both the underpinnings and many of the core components we prize today have actually been around a lot longer than most think.

We'll examine key developments across five distinct eras: Early Foundations (pre-1950), Symbolic AI (1950–1980), the rise of Machine Learning (1980–2000), the expansion of Data-Driven AI (2000–2010), and the explosive growth of Deep Learning and Generative AI (2010–today).

The Early Foundations (Pre-1950)

Artificial Intelligence, as we understand it today, is rooted in the intellectual soil of mathematics, logic, and wartime necessity. The ideas that would fuel the field of AI date back much earlier than the 1956 Dartmouth project.

One of the most influential thinkers was Alan Turing, whose work during World War II set the stage for modern computing and artificial intelligence. Turing's famous thought experiment—the Turing Test—offered a simple but powerful question: Can a machine's responses be indistinguishable from a human? The Turing Test became the philosophical benchmark for artificial intelligence: If a machine could convince a human that it was human, had it achieved intelligence?

During World War II, Turing worked at Bletchley Park in the UK's top-secret codebreaking unit. There, he helped design the Bombe, an early electro-mechanical computer used to decipher the encrypted messages sent by Nazi Germany's Enigma machine. This work was credited with shortening the war by years and saving millions of lives. It also marked a turning point—computers could solve problems that were previously considered the exclusive domain of human intelligence.

Meanwhile, in the United States, engineers and mathematicians like John von Neumann and Norbert Wiener made breakthroughs that deeply influenced early computing and AI theory. Von Neumann developed the architecture used in most modern computers, while Wiener's work on cybernetics laid the groundwork for feedback loops and control systems still used in robotics and autonomous systems today.

This period also saw massive government investments in computing infrastructure as part of military and defense initiatives. These investments accelerated the development of computers like the ENIAC (Electronic Numerical Integrator and Computer) in 1945, the first general-purpose programmable computer developed at the University of Pennsylvania.

While no modern AI companies emerged in this era, the foundational technologies and theories—logic, computation, and statistical analysis—set the stage for what was to come. Military necessity drove funding and urgency, but what emerged was a broader belief: machines could be taught to reason.

Symbolic AI (1950–1980)

The term "artificial intelligence" is credited to John McCarthy. It was during the famous Dartmouth Summer Research Project on Artificial Intelligence, as mentioned earlier, where AI had its founding moment. The project brought together leading thinkers such as Marvin Minsky, Claude Shannon, and Herbert Simon to explore whether machines could simulate every aspect of human learning and intelligence.

This era focused primarily on symbolic AI, or "good old-fashioned AI" (GOFAI), which used explicit rules and logic to manipulate symbols and solve problems. Researchers believed that if intelligence could be described in formal logic, then machines could be built to replicate it. The goal was to hard-code intelligence using if-then rules and structured problem-solving. An example of this kind of logic is: *If* the temperature is below 50°F, *then* suggest wearing a jacket.

One of the central figures of this period was Marvin Minsky, a cognitive scientist and co-founder of the MIT Artificial Intelligence Laboratory. Minsky was instrumental in shaping early AI theory, most notably through his development of *frames* and the *Society of Mind* theory. *Frames* introduced a method for representing knowledge in structured units or "schemas" that allowed AI systems to understand context by associating information with typical situations—such as what happens in a restaurant or at a doctor's visit. This provided a foundational approach to how machines might organize and retrieve knowledge like humans. His *Society of Mind* theory, published as a book in 1986, proposed that human intelligence is not the result of a single unified process, but rather a collection of smaller, interacting agents—each responsible for a different aspect of cognition. This radical idea offered a blueprint for how AI could simulate aspects of human thought by assembling networks of simpler sub-processes. Beyond his theoretical contributions, Minsky had an eclectic personality and a wide range of interests. He was passionate about music and even co-invented the first virtual reality head-mounted display in the 1960s, reflecting his relentless curiosity about how humans perceive and interact with the world.

Despite the early enthusiasm, symbolic AI encountered serious limitations. Programs that performed well in controlled environments—such as playing chess or solving algebra problems—struggled with the messiness of the real world. These systems lacked the ability to learn from experience or handle ambiguity. As expectations soared but results lagged, AI entered what became known as the first "AI winter" in the late 1970s, marked by a sharp decline in funding and interest.

Still, this era laid important foundations. Expert systems like DENDRAL and MYCIN emerged, applying rule-based reasoning to fields like chemistry and medicine. Early AI companies such as Symbolics and Lisp Machines Inc. began developing specialized hardware and software to support AI research.

Meanwhile, societal developments such as the Space Race and Cold War intensified interest in machine intelligence. Governments funneled research dollars into areas they believed would deliver technological superiority. As a result, early AI labs at Stanford, MIT, and Carnegie Mellon became breeding grounds for both theoretical breakthroughs and practical experimentation.

The symbolic AI era demonstrated both the promise and peril of rigid, rules-based intelligence. While its limitations ultimately ushered in new approaches, it firmly established AI as a legitimate, if challenging, field of scientific and commercial inquiry.

1980–2000: The First Wave of Machine Learning and the Birth of the Internet

The period from 1980 to 2000 was a turning point in AI and machine learning, marked by the transition from theoretical exploration to practical experimentation. While many AI dreams remained unrealized due to computational limits, this era laid the groundwork for the AI breakthroughs of the 21st century. It also overlapped with one of the most significant developments in human communication and commerce: the rise of the internet and the birth of the World Wide Web.

Machine Learning Advances

By the early 1980s, computer scientists were moving beyond symbolic AI and experimenting with statistical methods that would form the foundation of modern machine learning. These methods didn't rely on hardcoded rules but instead learned patterns from data, allowing them to improve performance over time. Among the techniques gaining traction were decision trees, support vector machines, Bayesian networks, and early neural networks.

Support vector machines worked by finding the best possible dividing line between different groups of data—like drawing a boundary to separate apples from oranges based on characteristics. Bayesian networks brought probability into the picture, helping machines make educated guesses in uncertain situations, such as diagnosing an illness based on symptoms. Neural networks mimicked how the human brain works, using layers of virtual "neurons" to recognize patterns in data. A major breakthrough in training these networks came through a method called backpropagation, where the system learned from its mistakes by adjusting how much importance it gave to different inputs—gradually getting better with each attempt.

Key researchers like Geoffrey Hinton, Judea Pearl, and Yann LeCun were instrumental in advancing these technologies. Hinton, often called one of the "godfathers" of deep learning, helped refine neural networks and popularized backpropagation, making them practical for real-world use. Pearl's work on reasoning with uncertainty through Bayesian networks laid the groundwork for systems that could make decisions in complex, imperfect environments. Together, their contributions helped shift AI from abstract theory to tools that could begin solving meaningful problems in fields like healthcare, robotics, and finance.

Companies like IBM, Xerox PARC, Bell Labs, and later Microsoft advanced both research and infrastructure. IBM's work in expert systems continued through the 1980s, while Microsoft began developing the ecosystem that would power personal computing and software-based business productivity tools—paving the way for digital transformation in the coming decades.

The Arrival of the Internet

While AI made steady strides during this era, the truly explosive force of innovation came from the emergence of the internet—and specifically, the World Wide Web.

At the center of this shift was Tim Berners-Lee, a British computer scientist who, in 1989 while working at CERN (the European Organization for Nuclear Research), proposed a system for sharing information among researchers using a networked protocol. By 1990, he had developed the first version of what would become the World Wide Web, including a browser (WorldWideWeb), the first website, and the foundational architecture: HTTP, HTML, and URLs.

Berners-Lee's invention was not the internet itself (which had its roots in ARPANET and U.S. military-funded networking efforts from the 1960s and 1970s), but rather the application layer that made it useful to everyday users and businesses. The Web provided a unified way to access and share documents globally. For this reason, he is widely credited with inventing the World Wide Web, and his vision of an open, decentralized web helped set the tone for a more democratized information ecosystem.

In 1993, the launch of the Mosaic browser—and later, Netscape Navigator—triggered a massive expansion of web usage. Companies like Yahoo, Amazon (1994), eBay (1995), and Google (1998) emerged during this period, altering how commerce, media, and communication functioned through this day. Quickly flashing back to our Chapter 2 discussion on endurance, these are certainly companies remembered 30-years later.

Among these, Yahoo was one of the first truly dominant internet companies. Founded in 1994 by Stanford graduate students Jerry Yang and David Filo, Yahoo began as a web directory—a manually curated index of websites that made the fledgling web more navigable. It quickly evolved into a full-fledged portal, offering search, email, news, weather, finance, and more. Yahoo's strength lay in its ability to become a gateway to the internet, effectively owning the home page for millions of users around the world.

Yahoo's success was driven by a blend of editorial curation, early search capability, and aggressive product expansion. It acquired dozens of companies in the late 1990s, including GeoCities and Broadcast.com (for which it paid nearly $6 billion), in an effort to expand its footprint in content and services. By 2000, Yahoo was the most visited website in the world, serving as the default internet experience for a large portion of the global population. Its influence in shaping the early consumer internet cannot be overstated—it became one of the first major digital advertising platforms, helped popularize personalized content delivery, and established early models of internet monetization that others would emulate.

Economic and Business Impact

By the late 1990s, the internet was already reshaping global economics. Between 1995 and 2000, the internet contributed approximately $300 billion to the U.S. economy, and by 2001, internet-related businesses accounted for over 5% of U.S. GDP. These numbers would grow exponentially in the decades to come.

The web allowed businesses to do things that were previously unimaginable:

- Reach global customers through e-commerce and digital marketing.

- Lower operating costs by automating supply chains and customer service.

- Create digital platforms that generated new business models—such as SaaS (Software as a Service), online advertising, and marketplaces.

- Enable small businesses to compete globally without needing physical storefronts.

Perhaps most importantly, the Web created the infrastructure upon which modern AI would thrive—providing massive data streams, connected platforms, and the demand for personalization and automation.

Despite the explosive growth of the internet, machine learning still faced limitations. Data was growing but remained relatively small compared to modern standards. Computational resources—especially GPUs and cloud computing—were not yet readily available. As a result, many promising techniques couldn't scale. Algorithms worked in theory or small datasets, but real-world application remained limited.

Nonetheless, this era produced the intellectual and technical DNA that would fuel the AI revolution in the 2000s and beyond.

2000–2010: The Rise of Data, the Web 2.0 Revolution, and the Foundations of Modern Machine Learning

The early 2000s marked a new chapter in artificial intelligence—a chapter fueled by the explosion of digital data and the increasing sophistication of computational power. In this decade, the building blocks of what we now recognize as modern AI began to take shape. At the center of this shift was the rise of machine learning (ML), fueled by breakthroughs in algorithms, the abundance of digital data, and improvements in hardware infrastructure.

One of the most critical enablers of this period was the emergence of big data—the vast and exponentially growing datasets generated by websites, social media platforms, e-commerce, and mobile devices. Big data gave machine learning models the material they needed to improve accuracy, make predictions, and deliver real-world applications. Simply put, big data made modern AI possible. By analyzing millions or even billions of data points, systems could begin to identify patterns and associations that were previously hidden.

Another foundational technology was natural language processing (NLP)—a field of AI focused on enabling machines to understand and generate human language. NLP is what powers language translation apps, digital assistants like Siri and Alexa, and even predictive text in messaging. During this decade, researchers made significant progress in creating systems that could not only parse text but also begin to infer meaning and intent.

Computer vision, another vital branch of AI, also began maturing in this era. Computer vision allows machines to analyze and understand images and videos—such as recognizing faces, reading license plates, or detecting anomalies in X-rays. This decade saw early success in object recognition and image classification, opening the door for applications in everything from security to healthcare.

A third major area was neural networks, inspired by the structure of the human brain. These models are composed of interconnected nodes (or "neurons") that work together to analyze input and produce output. Neural networks had been around since the 1950s, but it was in this era—thanks to better data and faster GPUs—that they started to show practical promise in fields like speech recognition and early image recognition. One especially important development was the concept of deep learning, which involved stacking multiple layers of neurons to create deep neural networks capable of learning complex patterns.

Key figures emerged during this time to push these innovations forward. Geoffrey Hinton, often referred to as the "Godfather of Deep Learning," made critical contributions in the development of deep neural networks. Hinton, a professor at the University of Toronto, co-invented the backpropagation algorithm—a method that allows neural networks to learn from their errors, and was previously referenced in this chapter. In 2006, Hinton and his collaborators published a landmark paper on deep belief networks, reigniting interest in neural networks and laying the groundwork for the next AI boom.

Yoshua Bengio, another Canadian researcher and a professor at the University of Montreal, worked closely on deep learning and neural networks. Bengio's work focused on representation learning—the idea that machines could learn useful features from raw data without requiring human-defined rules. His research helped systems become more adaptive and better at generalizing from examples.

The period also witnessed the ascent of disruptive companies that harnessed these technologies to change how businesses operated and how consumers interacted with digital platforms.

Google transformed itself from a search engine to an early AI powerhouse, leveraging big data and machine learning to power everything from search algorithms to targeted advertising. The introduction of Google Translate and the acquisition of key AI startups signaled the company's aggressive investment in machine learning.

Amazon revolutionized e-commerce through its recommendation engine, which used collaborative filtering algorithms to personalize product suggestions for users. This application of machine learning significantly increased customer engagement and revenue.

Netflix disrupted traditional media by using machine learning to recommend content, analyze viewer behavior, and optimize streaming performance. Its 2006 Netflix Prize—offering $1 million to improve its recommendation algorithm—galvanized the data science community and marked a turning point in commercial AI adoption.

Facebook, founded in 2004, began using machine learning to optimize user feeds, suggest connections, and serve more relevant ads. Its success at personalizing user experiences underscored the commercial power of data and algorithms.

These companies were not just using machine learning as a feature—they were building their business models around it. By leveraging early AI to make sense of big data, improve user experiences, and optimize operations, they set the tone for how AI would be adopted in the enterprise world.

Still, the technology had limitations as did the companies putting it to use. Moreover, while consumers and businesses saw indirect benefit from the propagation of AI, like finding a movie quicker on an emerging streaming platform, little had changed about how business got work done. And, despite promising advancements, most AI models required large labeled datasets, struggled with bias, and lacked explainability. Real-time decision-making and generalization across domains remained difficult. Yet, the groundwork had been laid for a future where AI would be central—not peripheral—to business strategy, and for the breakthrough decade that would follow.

2011–Today: The Deep Learning Revolution and the Age of Scaled AI

The period from 2011 to today marks a defining era in artificial intelligence—where breakthroughs in algorithms, data availability, and compute power ushered in the age of scaled AI. It was no longer about experiments in research labs. AI became a mainstream, industrial force reshaping how societies function, how businesses operate, and how individuals create, learn, and communicate.

From Artificial Intelligence to Deep Learning

Artificial Intelligence, as a discipline, had long sought to replicate or simulate human intelligence. But its progress had been hampered by limitations in data, hardware, and algorithmic scalability. That changed with the rise of deep learning.

Deep learning is a subfield of AI that uses artificial neural networks with many layers (hence "deep") to model and understand complex data patterns. These systems learn by example—feeding in massive datasets and adjusting internal parameters through training algorithms until the model can generalize and make accurate predictions. Deep learning excels in areas like speech recognition, image classification, language translation, and now even reasoning and coding.

This paradigm shift was largely ignited in 2012, when Geoffrey Hinton, Alex Krizhevsky, and Ilya Sutskever developed AlexNet, a convolutional neural network that drastically improved accuracy in the ImageNet competition—a benchmark for computer vision. Their work proved that deeper networks, when combined with GPUs and large datasets, could outperform previous AI systems by orders of magnitude.

Hinton continued to contribute to neural network research while mentoring many of the future pioneers of the modern AI movement. His students went on to lead groundbreaking work at institutions like Google Brain and OpenAI. Alongside Hinton, Yoshua Bengio in Canada and Yann LeCun in the U.S. contributed heavily to the theoretical and practical frameworks for deep learning. LeCun, for instance, led AI efforts at Facebook (now Meta), while Bengio continued to drive innovation at MILA, a prominent AI research institute in Montreal.

OpenAI, ChatGPT, and the Rise of LLMs

While deep learning had already proven its value in domains like computer vision and speech recognition, a new frontier emerged in the late 2010s: language. The development of Large Language Models (LLMs)—massive neural networks trained on billions or trillions of words—transformed natural language processing into one of AI's most powerful and accessible tools.

At the forefront of this revolution was OpenAI, a San Francisco-based research lab founded in 2015 by Elon Musk, Sam Altman, Ilya Sutskever, and others. OpenAI set out with a mission to ensure artificial intelligence benefits all of humanity, and to that end, began developing increasingly powerful models of natural language.

Their 2020 release of GPT-3 (Generative Pre-trained Transformer 3) shocked the world. GPT-3 was a 175-billion-parameter model capable of answering questions, writing essays, generating code, translating languages, simulating dialogue, and much more—all with remarkable fluency. The real magic of GPT-3 was its zero-shot and few-shot learning: users could prompt it with just a few examples, and it would infer how to complete tasks without retraining.

In 2022, OpenAI launched ChatGPT, a chat-based interface for interacting with its underlying LLMs. This product turned abstract capabilities into a familiar form: a chatbot that could respond intelligently to questions, write long-form responses, and assist with creative, technical, and educational tasks. It brought LLMs from the realm of research and niche API integrations into the daily experience of millions of users.

ChatGPT's viral success sparked widespread interest in LLMs across industries—from education to customer service to software development. Its impact inspired companies like Google (PaLM, Bard/Gemini), Meta (LLaMA), Anthropic (Claude), and Mistral to accelerate their development of foundation models. Microsoft, through its multi-billion dollar partnership with OpenAI, integrated GPT into its Office products, Azure cloud platform, and GitHub Copilot (an AI-powered code assistant).

What Are LLMs and Why Do They Matter?

A Large Language Model (LLM) is a deep learning model trained on massive text datasets—from books and websites to forums, Wikipedia, news articles, and more. It learns the statistical patterns of language—how words and phrases relate to each other—so that when you prompt it with a question or request, it can generate coherent, contextually relevant responses.

LLMs don't "understand" language like humans do. They are probabilistic pattern engines, generating the next most likely word based on the prompt and their training. But their size and training allow them to mimic understanding surprisingly well.

Key capabilities include:

- Text generation (emails, blogs, scripts, essays)

- Summarization of long documents or transcripts

- Translation between languages

- Question answering and research assistance

- Code generation and debugging

- Conversational AI for customer service or internal support

- Semantic search and knowledge extraction

These capabilities make LLMs incredibly versatile across business, education, and personal productivity. They eliminate time-consuming tasks, offer creative inspiration, and provide real-time assistance—empowering users to work faster, smarter, and often with fewer resources. Because they do not understand words, however, they are also not without error—or to what many describe as 'hallucinations.

AI in Devices and Consumer Experiences

At the same time, AI's presence in consumer devices surged. Edge AI—machine learning that runs locally on devices rather than in the cloud—

enabled smartphones, laptops, smart home systems, and wearables to perform real-time inference and personalization.

Some common examples:

- Facial recognition for unlocking devices or authenticating payments

- Predictive text and grammar correction in mobile keyboards

  - Health tracking with intelligent analysis of biometrics like heart rate or sleep patterns

- Camera enhancements through AI-driven image processing

- On-device voice assistants (Siri, Google Assistant) that respond to commands even without internet connectivity

Companies like Apple, Samsung, Google, and Huawei embedded AI chips directly into their hardware (e.g., Apple's Neural Engine or Google's Tensor SoC), enabling efficient performance and privacy-preserving computation. As of the final editing of this book, OpenAI and renowned Apple product designer Jony Ive have announced a partnership to develop AI-centric personal devices. AI continues to evolve, minute by minute.

Business Impact and the Disconnect

Despite the immense potential of artificial intelligence—especially the transformative power of large language models (LLMs)—most businesses have experienced its benefits in limited, fragmented ways. While LLMs and machine learning tools have become increasingly common, they are often deployed as add-ons to existing platforms, rather than integrated from the ground up.

AI as an Add-On, Not a Core Strategy

Major software providers like Salesforce, Microsoft, and Bloomberg have made substantial investments in embedding AI into their existing ecosystems. For example:

• Salesforce Einstein brought predictive analytics, natural language processing, and AI-generated insights to customer relationship management (CRM). It allowed users to receive recommendations on lead prioritization, opportunity scoring, and email personalization—without ever leaving their Salesforce dashboard.

• Microsoft Copilot, integrated into Microsoft 365, enabled users to generate text in Word, build data visualizations in Excel, summarize emails in Outlook, and brainstorm ideas in PowerPoint. These capabilities marked a leap forward in personal productivity, powered by OpenAI's GPT models.

• BloombergGPT, a domain-specific LLM trained on financial data, began transforming the Bloomberg Terminal, allowing financial professionals to parse filings, summarize earnings reports, generate analyst notes, and interact with structured financial data in new ways.

These integrations were meaningful—they brought the power of LLMs to millions of business users. However, they also shared a key limitation: they were "bolted onto" legacy systems.

Salesforce, Microsoft 365, and the Bloomberg Terminal are all platforms that originated in the 1980s or 1990s. Their architectures were not designed with AI as a foundational layer. As a result, the AI capabilities introduced into these platforms often functioned as enhancements rather than transformations. They provided incremental productivity gains, but not a redefinition of how work gets done.

The Resulting Fragmentation

Even as AI made its way into enterprise software, the broader business ecosystem remained disconnected:

• Marketing teams used AI for content creation in tools like Jasper or Canva, but tracked performance separately in Google Analytics or HubSpot.

• Sales teams might receive predictive lead scoring in Salesforce but manually update other CRMs or BI tools.

• Operations automated workflows in Zapier or UIPath but couldn't connect directly to finance or inventory systems.

• Legal and HR teams relied on AI-powered contract summarizers or policy generators that didn't integrate with internal compliance tools or document management systems.

This siloed ecosystem created a paradox: AI was everywhere, but its impact was scattered. Each department had access to smart tools, but the tools didn't speak to each other. The intelligence was surface-level—useful in isolation, but lacking the cross-functional context needed to drive real transformation.

Security, Governance, and the Small Business Gap

The scattered nature of AI adoption introduced serious concerns around data privacy, model transparency, and control:

- Many tools routed proprietary business data through third-party integration tools (known as APIs) with unclear data retention policies.

- LLM providers, in some cases, retained prompts and outputs for training future models, creating IP exposure and compliance risks.

- There were limited safeguards for aligning AI outputs with internal governance standards, particularly in regulated industries like finance, healthcare, or legal.

For large enterprises, these risks were managed through internal AI governance boards, dedicated IT/security teams, and complex vendor assessments, even within an environment where the ethical considerations remained less than fully defined as you recall from Chapter 3. But for small and mid-sized businesses, these barriers were often insurmountable. AI became something only large firms could afford to use securely and at scale.

Even when small businesses were willing to invest, they faced another challenge: complexity. To stitch together a usable AI solution, they needed to:

- Manage multiple vendors and pricing tiers.

- Train staff on half a dozen platforms.

- Build APIs or no-code integrations across software that was never meant to work together.

- Maintain security and compliance across decentralized systems.

For many, the promise of AI remained just out of reach—visible in demos, but elusive in practice.

A Shift Toward Intelligence at the Core

As AI adoption matured, businesses began to realize that the future was not in layering AI on top of legacy systems, but in building platforms where AI is embedded at the core—from architecture to user interface to outcomes.

That realization led to the emergence of new categories, such as the Intelligent Business Management Platform™ (IBMP)—a system built not just to house AI tools, but to operationalize AI as a default way of working.

Rather than treating AI as a feature, the IBMP treats it as a foundation.

In this model:

- Data is centralized, siloed for security, and owned by the business—not shared with outside LLMs.

- AI Tasks (intelligent agents) are used to perform real business functions—sales prospecting, document review, financial reconciliation—not just to write content.

- Workflows are chat-driven and human-friendly, replacing dropdown-heavy interfaces with natural conversation.

- One-click activation allows any business, no matter how small, to deploy enterprise-grade AI without months of configuration.

This is the vision behind our core product LIBBi, for example—the world's first Intelligent Business Management Platform™. LIBBi wasn't created to enhance outdated software. It was created to replace it—to serve as a single, secure, and intelligent operating system for modern business.

And in doing so, it closes the loop on what has, until now, been a disconnected AI landscape.

As we stand in the present, we are living through a moment as significant as the invention of the internet. AI is no longer optional—it's a strategic necessity. Businesses that ignore AI risk irrelevance, while those that adopt recklessly risk ethical, financial, and reputational damage.

From 2011 to today, the AI world has shifted from possibility to presence. What began as academic models is now embedded in everyday business decisions, customer experiences, and human creativity. And as we look forward to the next chapter, the question is no longer, *"Will AI transform business?"* but *"How will you use it to transform yours?"*

Final Thoughts: From Fragmentation to Foundation — Paving the Way to Intelligent Integration

The evolution of artificial intelligence from theoretical thought experiments to an operational force in modern business has been anything but linear. From the intellectual explorations of Alan Turing and Marvin Minsky to the statistical innovations of Hinton, Bengio, and LeCun, and finally to the mainstream deployment of LLMs by OpenAI and others, AI has continuously transformed itself in response to both technological progress and societal need. We have moved from symbolic rule-based systems to scalable neural networks and now to generative systems that simulate reasoning, communication, and creativity.

Yet, despite remarkable technological milestones, the application of AI within businesses has largely been fragmented—spread across tools, departments, and platforms that do not communicate or integrate well. While companies like Salesforce, Microsoft, and Bloomberg have made meaningful strides to embed AI within their legacy ecosystems, their efforts often stop short of full operational transformation. In reality, these AI additions have functioned more like powerful appendages than integrated brains, extending existing workflows but not fundamentally reshaping them.

That reshaping is now underway.

The emergence of the Intelligent Business Management Platform™ (IBMP), as an example, signals a paradigm shift. No longer must businesses choose between complexity and intelligence. With AI at the foundation, not just at the edge, businesses can operate in ways that are simpler, faster, more secure, and more human-centered than ever before. The IBMP represents a unification of AI capabilities under a single roof: centralized data, one-click AI tasks, chat-based execution, and full transparency. This is not a future vision. It is the new standard for what business software must become.

As we close this chapter on where we are now in the AI business landscape, we turn our attention to where we go from here. Chapter 4 will explore the leadership required to harness this new era—how business leaders can align strategy, culture, and execution to not only adopt AI, but to lead through it. Because just as technology evolves, so must the people who wield it. And in an age where intelligence is embedded into every system, the most critical decisions still rest in human hands.

Chapter 4: Core AI Categories – From Foundational Technologies to Practical Applications

In 2023, a small logistics company in the Midwest—let's call it Titan Freight—was running out of runway. Legacy systems, rising customer expectations, and shrinking margins were squeezing the life out of their operations. Dispatchers managed routes on paper logs. Finance lived in spreadsheets. Customer service answered the same twelve questions, every single day.

During a leadership meeting, the CEO paused and posed a question that would quietly shape their future:

"What if every department had a second brain?"

They didn't use the term "AI." They didn't know what an LLM was. They weren't chasing tech trends. What they were looking for—though they didn't quite have the language—was intelligent support. Not a replacement for their team, but something to make their tools smarter, their decisions faster, and their customer experience better.

Two years later, Titan Freight had quietly transformed. Task-based AI agents were embedded across operations, finance, sales, and support. The results weren't dramatic because the technology was flashy. They were dramatic because it was finally practical.

That's the journey this chapter explores: the shift from AI as an abstract concept to AI as a useful tool—not someday, but now.

If Chapter 3 was a high-speed tour through the history of artificial intelligence, this chapter slows down and zooms in. Here, we focus on how modern AI works, what categories it falls into, where it's being deployed, and what limitations still remain.

No PhD required. No jargon necessary. Just a working understanding of how today's AI—generative tools, LLMs, agents, and orchestrated systems—actually function in the real world, especially within the growing framework of the Intelligent Business Management Platform™.

If you've ever asked yourself *What can AI actually do for my business?*, you're in the right place.

Let's move from what AI is—to what it does.

Simple AI: Rules-Based and Narrow in Scope

At its most fundamental level, artificial intelligence doesn't require learning models or advanced algorithms. Sometimes, intelligence is simply structure—a system of predefined logic that responds consistently to known conditions. These systems, known as rules-based AI or expert systems, operate on basic "if this, then that" instructions. They don't learn. They don't adapt. But in the right context, they don't need to.

In fact, this kind of logic-driven AI has quietly powered business automation for decades. From inventory management triggers to customer service chat flows, rules-based systems have delivered speed, consistency, and cost savings long before today's neural networks took the spotlight.

And while they may not feel intelligent by today's standards, they demonstrate an important principle that still applies: AI doesn't always have to be complex to be useful.

Example: Zendesk Macros and Triggers

Customer support platforms like Zendesk use rules-based AI to streamline operations. With Zendesk, businesses can set up macros (predefined responses) and triggers (automated actions based on specific conditions). For instance, when a customer submits a support ticket containing the phrase "password reset," Zendesk can automatically send a templated response and categorize the ticket. No learning or adaptation is taking place—but it's fast, reliable, and reduces the workload for human agents.

These systems are great for routine tasks and environments where predictability is high. However, they lack the flexibility or reasoning of more advanced AI types. As businesses seek to handle more nuanced customer needs or data-heavy workflows, simple AI often becomes the first step on a larger AI adoption journey.

Generative AI: From Content Creation to Intelligent Interfaces

Generative AI refers to artificial intelligence systems that can create new content—text, images, audio, code, and more—rather than just analyzing or categorizing existing data. Unlike rules-based or predictive systems, generative AI uses advanced models trained on massive datasets to simulate creativity, language, and reasoning.

The foundational breakthrough behind most generative AI systems is the Large Language Model (LLM), as previously introduced. LLMs are deep learning models trained on billions or even trillions of words. Their purpose is to learn the statistical structure of language well enough to generate coherent, contextually relevant responses based on input prompts. In essence, every time you use a generative AI tool to write an article, generate code, or summarize a document, you're interacting with a type of LLM under the hood.

Examples of Generative AI in Action

- ChatGPT (OpenAI) – The most recognized consumer-facing generative AI tool, ChatGPT uses the GPT-3.5 or GPT-4 model to generate human-like responses to a wide range of prompts, from writing stories to solving technical problems.
- GitHub Copilot (powered by OpenAI) – A generative AI assistant for software developers that suggests code completions and even full functions based on natural language input.
- Jasper – A marketing-focused platform that uses generative AI to help businesses create blog posts, social media captions, ads, and more.
- DALL·E (OpenAI) and Midjourney – These generative visual models can create unique images based on text prompts, widely used in advertising, media, and design.
- Notion AI – Integrated directly into the Notion workspace app, this tool helps users summarize meeting notes, draft memos, and enhance productivity through generative suggestions.
- Canva Magic Write – A creative writing tool within Canva that enables users to create copy for designs and presentations using AI.
- Microsoft 365 Copilot – Embedded into Word, Excel, and Outlook, Copilot uses generative AI to assist with document drafting, summarizing emails, creating reports, and even generating charts based on natural language.

These products do not just "use AI"—they actively create new content in response to user instructions, making them fundamentally different from traditional analytics or automation tools.

These LLMs are trained on a combination of internet text, public repositories, books, code, news, and more. Through billions of examples, they learn the complex patterns in human communication—enabling everything from summarizing legal documents to designing graphics from scratch.

Why Generative AI Matters

Generative AI enables a new kind of productivity—one rooted not in automation of fixed processes, but in real-time, creative augmentation. For businesses, this means:

- Rapid creation of personalized content at scale
- Human-like assistance in email, presentations, and customer responses
- On-demand generation of visual assets, code, or product concepts
- Language-based access to structured knowledge

And yet, while generative AI is a leap forward, it is not without limitations— hallucinations, data privacy concerns, model bias, and integration complexity. These issues set the stage for the next category: AI Agents and Tasks, where generative capabilities are directed toward structured, outcomes-driven workflows.

While generative AI currently represents the most visible and commercially adopted class of advanced intelligence, the frontier of artificial intelligence is already expanding into even more ambitious territory. Artificial General Intelligence (AGI), long considered the "holy grail" of AI, aspires to match or exceed human cognitive abilities across any task or domain. Unlike generative models that excel in narrow applications, AGI would possess reasoning, learning, memory, and adaptability equivalent to or surpassing human intellect. In parallel, hybrid multimodal systems are emerging—AI models capable of understanding and synthesizing information from multiple sources at once, such as text, images, audio, and spatial data. These systems signal a move beyond single-domain intelligence toward more contextually aware, environment-interactive AI. Technologies like GPT-4o, Gemini 1.5, and Meta's LLaVA illustrate early steps in this evolution. Additionally, autonomous AI agents or AI Tasks and orchestration frameworks like AutoGPT and CrewAI are pushing models to not just respond—but act. These next-generation capabilities will be explored in greater depth in Chapter 5, where we turn our attention to the horizon of AI: what's coming, who is building it, and how leaders must prepare for a world where intelligence itself becomes a platform.

LLM Wrappers: Convenience Without Core Capability

As large language models (LLMs) like GPT-4, Claude, Gemini, and Mistral have become increasingly powerful, a wave of startups and enterprise tools has emerged offering customized interfaces that make these models easier to use. These tools are commonly known as LLM wrappers—platforms that "wrap" an existing LLM inside a user-friendly interface or workflow, often targeting a specific business need.

What Is an LLM Wrapper?

An LLM wrapper is a software application that connects to a foundational LLM (via API) and provides an enhanced user experience without altering the model itself. Most wrappers offer features such as:

- A simplified interface (chat, form-based prompt builder, dashboard)
- Pre-configured prompt templates or workflows
- API integrations with productivity or enterprise tools (e.g., Google Docs, Notion, Salesforce, Slack)
- Task chaining or light automation of multiple LLM calls

What these wrappers do *not* do is modify the LLM's underlying architecture, retrain it, or make it more intelligent. They offer a layer of usability—not foundational advancement.

Product Examples:

Some of the most well-known LLM wrappers include:

- Jasper AI – A content generation platform that wraps GPT-4 and other LLMs to help marketers and writers quickly produce blog posts, product descriptions, and ad copy using templated prompts and tone-of-voice controls.
- Copy.ai – Similar to Jasper, Copy.ai provides structured templates for sales emails, LinkedIn posts, and product messaging by wrapping GPT-based models for commercial copywriting.
- ChatGPT Enterprise – While built by OpenAI, this enterprise version functions as a secure wrapper that adds admin controls, SOC

2 compliance, business-specific integrations, and dedicated support for corporate deployment.

- Fireflies.ai – An AI meeting assistant that wraps LLMs for transcribing, summarizing, and extracting action items from meetings on Zoom, Teams, and Google Meet. The intelligence comes from the LLMs; the value comes from integration and formatting.
- Legal Robot – A domain-specific wrapper used in legal tech that provides contract review, clause extraction, and risk analysis using LLMs trained or fine-tuned for legal language.

These examples show that LLM wrappers can be helpful in automating tasks, reducing human input, or creating niche workflows, but the intelligence is still inherited—not invented.

Why They Exist:

Wrappers proliferated because foundational LLMs—while powerful—can be difficult to use effectively, especially for non-technical professionals. Wrappers solve real problems by:

- Lowering the barrier to entry for businesses unfamiliar with prompt engineering or AI APIs
- Offering pre-built solutions for niche domains (e.g., blogging, legal review, sales outreach)
- Embedding language models into familiar work environments (e.g., Google Workspace, CRMs)

In this way, wrappers play a role similar to early graphical user interfaces (GUIs)—translating command-line power into accessible experiences for everyday users.

Despite their utility, LLM wrappers suffer from significant constraints:

- Redundancy: Many tools offer overlapping features with minimal differentiation—just new prompts, templates, or branding over the same core models.
- Vendor lock-in: Some wrappers restrict access to user data or offer little transparency into how LLMs process prompts, creating risk for sensitive business workflows.
- Limited customization: Since wrappers rely on third-party LLMs, businesses can't fully adapt the model to their specific data, compliance needs, or operational tone.
- Shallow integration: Most wrappers sit on top of workflows, rather than integrate deeply into operational systems like ERPs, proprietary databases, or internal APIs. They act more like "assistants" than full workflow participants.

Wrappers vs. Core Platforms

In essence, LLM wrappers help bridge the gap between foundational model capability and mainstream usability—but they are often temporary or superficial solutions. Unlike full fledged platforms, which embed AI functionality as a core architecture within a secure, integrated ecosystem, wrappers tend to enhance only the surface layer of a business's operations.

Embodied AI: Intelligence That Moves

While much of the attention in artificial intelligence has focused on models that generate text, images, or predictions, a distinct and vital category of AI exists—one that powers machines interacting with the physical world. This is known as Embodied AI.

Embodied AI refers to artificial intelligence systems integrated into robots, vehicles, drones, and other physical devices that perceive their environment and take action in real time. These systems combine perception, decision-making, and actuation, allowing machines to navigate, manipulate objects, and adapt to dynamic surroundings.

Unlike generative AI, which produces content based on patterns in language or images, embodied AI operates in the real world—interpreting sensor inputs, planning movements, and executing physical tasks. It often leverages components such as computer vision, reinforcement learning, and spatial reasoning, and must process real-time data from sources like cameras, LiDAR, ultrasonic sensors, and GPS.

Product Examples:

- Boston Dynamics' Spot uses embodied AI to walk, navigate stairs, and carry payloads in industrial environments.
- Tesla Autopilot and Waymo's autonomous vehicles employ embodied AI for real-time decision-making on roads, integrating object detection, path planning, and motion control.
- Amazon Robotics enables warehouse automation through fleets of intelligent machines that locate, retrieve, and transport inventory.
- Da Vinci Surgical System applies embodied AI to assist surgeons in performing precise, minimally invasive procedures.

While embodied AI can incorporate components of generative AI—such as conversational interfaces or vision-language models—its core is rooted in action. These systems must continually respond to complex, often unpredictable environments, making them uniquely challenging to build and train.

As we move into an era where intelligent machines not only think but also move, embodied AI will become increasingly essential across industries—from logistics and healthcare to construction and consumer robotics.

AI Agents and Tasks: The Action Layer of Artificial Intelligence

As artificial intelligence matures, it becomes increasingly important to distinguish between what AI is and what AI does. While terms like simple AI or generative AI describe the nature of the technology—its capabilities, models, or outputs—terms like AI agent or AI Task refer to how that technology is actually put to use. They represent the action layer of AI: systems designed to take initiative, make decisions, and execute on behalf of a human or business objective.

We use the terms AI Agent and AI Task interchangeably. Technically, they describe the same concept—a self-contained application of AI that completes a specific job or outcome. However, we've chosen to call them Tasks for an important reason: it emphasizes action. Unlike "agent," which can sound abstract or even anthropomorphic, "task" is concrete. Tasks get things done. They are not passive models waiting for prompts—they are purpose-built modules designed to deliver results.

What Is an AI Task?

An AI Task is a focused application of AI designed to solve a specific business problem or perform a specific business function. It may use language models, data analysis, external integrations (called APIs), or a combination of tools to achieve its goal. What distinguishes an AI Task from other forms of AI is its structure:

- It has a defined purpose and outcome (e.g., schedule meetings, generate sales leads, draft contracts).

- It often includes steps or logic that simulate decision-making and action.

- It can be triggered by humans or other systems, and it often returns a tangible result.

- It has been trained or enhanced to overcome the inconsistencies or known likely hallucinations that exist in various LLM's.

How AI Tasks Differ from Simple and Generative AI

To clarify their role, it's helpful to contrast AI Tasks with simpler or more general categories of AI that we have already talked about in this chapter. Specifically, Simple AI performs a single, repeatable function such as routing an email or recommending a product. It is rules-based or model-driven but lacks flexibility or context. Generative AI focuses on creating content: generating text, images, code, music, and more. It is most commonly associated with large language models (LLMs) like GPT-4, Claude, or Gemini. These models generate outputs based on prompts, but do not inherently structure those outputs for execution or workflow.

AI Tasks go a huge step further. They combine the intelligence of generative AI with real-world utility. Tasks embed logic, goals, and constraints. They are capable not only of generating content, but also of submitting forms, sending emails, triggering workflows, or requesting human input. They may access data systems, enforce compliance steps, or integrate directly into business operations.

In essence, AI Tasks turn intelligence into productivity.

Examples of How Businesses Use AI Tasks

To appreciate the value of AI Tasks, consider how real businesses use them to improve performance and scale their operations:

- Lead Generation Task
  A real estate firm uses an AI Task to scan public data, filter by property investment criteria, and generate personalized outreach emails to qualified owners. The task connects to a CRM, automates list building, drafts messages, and monitors replies.

- HR Onboarding Task
  An HR department uses an AI Task to onboard new employees. It generates welcome packets, configures accounts, and schedules meetings. It also answers questions using a chatbot trained on internal documents.

- Invoice Reconciliation Task
  A business uses an AI Task to match vendor invoices to purchase orders and receipts. It flags discrepancies, sends alerts, and drafts inquiries, allowing the finance team to focus on exceptions.

- Marketing Task
  A marketing director uses an AI Task to analyze performance data, recommend content strategies, and draft messaging. It schedules reviews and populates task lists in project tools.

- Load Matching Task

  A dispatcher or logistics coordinator uses an AI Task to match available truck drivers with active or incoming customer loads. The Task evaluates routes, equipment types, driver availability, and delivery windows. It recommends optimal driver-load pairings, notifies both parties, and automatically updates load boards and dispatch systems. With proper enhancement, it can even make the market between the shipper and the load hauler.

- Business Compliance Task
  A company uses an AI Task to track deadlines, prepare documentation, and ensure completeness of forms. It alerts teams when compliance actions are required.

These are just a few use cases, but they point to a much broader opportunity: AI Tasks offer modular, specialized, and scalable intelligence that plugs directly into how a business operates.

Why It Matters:

The rise of AI Tasks signals a shift in how we think about AI. It's not just a tool for discovery or creativity—it's becoming an operational partner. Unlike monolithic platforms, wrappers, or all-in-one tools, tasks are flexible. They can be deployed one at a time, customized for a department, or chained together to power full workflows.

As the AI landscape continues to evolve, the businesses that thrive won't just use AI—they'll deploy it in ways that align with their goals, values, and customers. That begins with understanding AI Tasks—and knowing what you want them to accomplish.

Vector Databases and Achieving Precision, Privacy, and Protection

As artificial intelligence has grown more powerful, so too has its appetite for data—particularly unstructured data like documents, images, and audio. Traditional databases are good at storing structured data (like rows in a spreadsheet), but they struggle to handle the types of complex information that modern AI models rely on. That's where vector databases come in.

What Is a Vector Database?

In simple terms, a vector database stores information as vectors—mathematical representations of data that capture meaning, similarity, and relationships between things. For example, instead of storing the word "apple" as just a string of letters, a vector database might store it as a multi-dimensional number that represents its similarity to "fruit," "tree," or "iPhone," depending on the context.

These systems are critical for powering features like:

- Semantic search: Finding documents based on meaning, not just keywords.

- Contextual recommendation engines: Suggesting products or content based on user behavior and intent.

- Retrieval-Augmented Generation (RAG): Supplementing AI prompts with relevant external information for more accurate answers.

Why They Matter

Vector databases are foundational to many advanced AI applications because they allow systems to retrieve information that is most relevant—even when it's not an exact match. This makes them ideal for tasks like legal document analysis, customer support, and intelligent decision-making.

But with that power comes risk. Storing sensitive business data in vectorized formats—especially if centralized or pooled for training—can lead to major privacy concerns. If the same vector database powers multiple clients or applications, there is a risk of unintentional data leakage, model drift, or even competitive exposure. As generative and agent-based AI becomes more embedded in operations, the data that fuels these systems becomes an even more critical asset.

In an AI landscape increasingly defined by who owns and controls the data, vector databases represent both an opportunity and a decision point. The best AI systems don't just process data well. They treat it with the respect it deserves. We'll discuss data security in a later chapter but, to plant a seed, getting this right is a vital element of any AI solution, especially ones used in your business.

As we've explored the core categories of artificial intelligence—from simple AI and generative models to advanced AI tasks—one pattern becomes clear: the true power of AI emerges not just from individual technologies, but from how they are integrated into business operations. While each AI tool serves a purpose, most businesses today face a bigger challenge: unifying these tools into a single, intelligent system that works in harmony.

An Emerging Solution and Case Study: The Intelligent Business Management Platform™

As generative AI tools and LLM wrappers have gained widespread attention, many businesses have experimented with artificial intelligence through tools for content creation, document summarization, and chat-based customer support. While these applications offer immediate productivity gains, they often function as isolated features added to legacy systems—systems that were not originally designed to support AI.

As a case study on an emerging solution, we further introduce the Intelligent Business Management Platform™ (IBMP), a new class of software as a service (SaaS) that integrates AI capabilities at the architectural level. Rather than layering intelligence onto existing tools, IBMPs are built from the ground up to serve as AI-native environments—unifying data, task execution, and user interaction through intelligent automation.

What Is an Intelligent Business Management Platform™?

An IBMP serves as a centralized system for AI-powered business operations. Unlike traditional SaaS applications that target narrow functions like accounting or HR, an IBMP is structured to support the entire enterprise. It combines natural language interfaces, AI task automation, generative content generation, and vector-based search within a single framework.

Core Attributes of an IBMP:

- Centralized and Siloed Data Ownership
  All business data—ranging from documents and customer records to financials and operations—is stored in a structured and isolated environment, where each business maintains exclusive ownership. This ensures privacy and prevents external LLMs from training on proprietary information.
- Unified Business Infrastructure
  IBMPs replace the need for separate CRM, ERP, communication, and project management tools. Instead of forcing integrations

between disparate systems, an IBMP offers a consistent environment where all functions are natively connected.

- AI Task Marketplace

  One of the defining features of an IBMP is its access to a marketplace of AI-powered Tasks or agents. These tasks automate functions across departments—from customer communication and financial analysis to onboarding and compliance. They can be deployed and customized through simple activation, often via a chat interface.

- Conversational Interfaces for Task Execution

  Rather than relying on forms and drop-down menus, IBMPs use natural language interfaces to let users interact with the platform. Employees can trigger workflows, generate reports, or update data simply by conversing with an AI assistant.

- Customer-Facing Intelligence

  An IBMP supports both internal users and external customers. Tools like smart intake forms, status dashboards, dynamic booking pages, and auto-generated communications can be personalized and updated in real time using AI.

- Rapid Onboarding and Low Friction Customization

  IBMPs are built for quick deployment and minimal reliance on technical teams. Businesses can go live in minutes and expand capabilities over time through intuitive interfaces and modular task components.

- Outcome-Driven Design

  IBMPs emphasize real business value—measured in time savings, revenue gains, risk reduction, and user satisfaction—rather than offering features for their own sake.

- Human-Centered and Transparent Operations

  AI processes are explainable by design. Business users retain control over workflows and decision-making, with visibility into how tasks are performed and data is used.

- Scalability Across Roles and Teams

  From small businesses to growing enterprises, IBMPs are structured to support multiple users, teams, and functions—allowing collaboration across departments within a shared intelligent framework.

Why This Category Is Timely

The adoption of generative AI tools has brought new capabilities to many businesses, but often in disjointed ways. Teams use one tool for generating content, another for managing analytics, and yet another for automation—leading to fragmented workflows and data silos. IBMPs offer a structural solution to this problem, embedding intelligence into the business's core rather than relying on external patches or third-party wrappers.

As the IBMP model gains traction, it represents one of the most integrated and holistic expressions of enterprise AI—offering businesses a unified environment where AI is not an add-on but a foundational capability.

Final Thoughts: From Understanding to Leadership

In the 1990s, IBM's Deep Blue faced off against world chess champion Garry Kasparov in a widely publicized series of matches. At first, Kasparov won decisively—his creative, intuitive play easily outmaneuvering the machine. But in 1997, Deep Blue returned, equipped with better algorithms, more processing power, and an army of human engineers fine-tuning its every move. This time, the machine won. The moment was more than symbolic. It marked a shift—not just in what machines could do, but in how humans would relate to intelligence that was not their own.

That same shift is now underway across every industry and business function.

As we've explored throughout this chapter, artificial intelligence is not one monolithic force, but a rapidly evolving landscape of models, architectures, and applications. From the reliability of simple AI to the generative power of large language models, from the flexibility of vector databases to the executional strength of AI Tasks, each innovation brings new capabilities—and new decisions. At the leading edge of change for business operations is the Intelligent Business Management Platform™—a new category that solves many of the challenges inherent in other AI solutions.

But as with Kasparov and Deep Blue, success doesn't come from resisting the machine—or blindly trusting it. It comes from learning to play a new kind of game.

Understanding these technologies, their roles, and their trade-offs is no longer a technical advantage—it's a leadership imperative. Businesses that thrive in this next era will be those that use AI not just widely, but wisely. They'll focus not just on what AI can do, but on what it should do—aligned with strategic goals, ethical commitments, and human values.

Chapter 3 gave us the historical lens. Chapter 4 offered the technical map.

In Chapter 5, we look forward at where AI is going. And, now, I suspect you'll have some predictions of your own.

Chapter 5: Five Years Forward – The Coming Wave

In 1995, Bill Gates wrote a now-famous memo titled *"The Internet Tidal Wave."* It wasn't flashy. It wasn't long. But it changed the trajectory of Microsoft—and, arguably, the internet itself. In it, Gates warned that the internet wasn't just a feature to be added. It was a paradigm shift—one that would reshape business, technology, and society.

"The Internet," he wrote, "is crucial to every part of our business."

At the time, many still viewed the internet as a novelty. Gates saw something different: a transformation so profound that any company slow to adapt would be left behind. Within months, Microsoft realigned its product roadmap, shifted its strategy, and reoriented around the web. That internal memo is now regarded as one of the most pivotal communications in modern business history.

Today, artificial intelligence is experiencing its own tidal wave.

But this wave isn't just about connectivity. It's about reasoning. About generation, automation, and decision-making. It's about systems that not only process, but learn. As we explored in Chapters 3 and 4, this wave isn't on the horizon. It's already here—at our feet.

Chapter 3 took us back—through the evolution of AI, from symbolic logic to neural networks to generative models like GPT. Chapter 4 brought us to now—unpacking the tools, language models, and AI agents shaping how work gets done. Together, they revealed the shape of this moment.

Now, we look forward.

In this chapter, we forecast what the next five years are likely to bring—and what it means for the organizations that intend not just to adapt, but to lead.

We'll explore:

- The rise of autonomous Tasks and AI-generated Tasks on demand.
- The accelerating path toward Artificial General Intelligence (AGI). The emergence of AI-native companies where Tasks drive execution.
- The role of governments, militaries, and nation-states in the AI race.
- The infrastructure boom—spanning chips, energy, and cloud—to power AI at scale.
- And the near-universal adoption of intelligent operating systems for business.

Like the internet in 1995, AI is reshaping the landscape.

But unlike 1995, this transformation is moving at exponential speed. Businesses won't have a decade to respond. Those who see the shift coming will help shape it. The rest will find themselves reacting to a world that moved without them.

This chapter is your briefing on what's next—and how to be ready for it.

The Rise of Fully Autonomous Tasks

As AI systems evolve beyond static outputs and predefined workflows, a new frontier is emerging: fully autonomous AI Tasks. These are not just tools that follow instructions—they are adaptive, goal-driven entities capable of initiating, planning, and completing complex tasks with minimal or no human intervention, growing on the AI Task capabilities that have emerged over the past year.

In today's systems, AI Tasks often assist with discrete functions—such as summarizing a document, responding to a customer inquiry, or automating an onboarding sequence. They're powerful, but they remain reactive: they wait for input. Fully autonomous agents are different. These systems observe, decide, and act, often in dynamic and unpredictable environments. They operate more like junior executives than digital assistants—evaluating changing conditions, coordinating across multiple systems, and sometimes even spawning sub-agents to carry out subtasks.

This concept is deeply connected to the long-standing vision of Artificial General Intelligence (AGI), discussed a bit later in this chapter, a form of AI that can understand, learn, and apply knowledge across a wide range of tasks at a human-like level. While AGI remains a future milestone, autonomous agents represent a practical and intermediate step toward that horizon. They are not "general" in the philosophical sense, but they are increasingly generalizable within specific business domains, capable of flexibly adapting to new inputs and goals.

One of the most compelling predictions in this space is the emergence of "self-constructing" AI Tasks—platforms where users can simply state a business objective ("I need a customer retention program," or "build a weekly financial dashboard from my billing data"), and the AI not only configures the task but selects the right data sources, constructs the workflow, deploys the interface, and begins execution autonomously. In this vision, the boundary between AI developer and AI user collapses, ushering in a world where anyone can command enterprise-level capabilities with natural language alone.

These agentic systems will require a shift in platform architecture. AI Tasks will need:

- Goal orientation (not just instructions)
- Memory and context-awareness (to operate across time and systems)
- Planning and reasoning frameworks (to break large goals into steps)
- Multi-agent orchestration (to delegate subtasks and synchronize execution)

In addition to our work at InChannel AI on this future innovation, projects like AutoGPT, CrewAI, and OpenAgents have begun to explore this terrain. However, their current limitations—such as reliability, interpretability, and data governance—highlight why business adoption at scale still requires frameworks like the Intelligent Business Management Platform™ (IBMP), introduced in the last chapter. A true IBMP will act as both the host and the regulator of autonomous AI Tasks, coordinating agents while ensuring security, compliance, and alignment with business strategy.

In the near future, business systems will not just respond to commands—they will propose solutions, identify opportunities, and execute strategies. The role of the human leader will shift from direct operator to strategic overseer: less about clicking and configuring, more about guiding, evaluating, and refining.

As we transition from AI as a feature to AI as a workforce, the rise of fully autonomous, agentic systems represents not just a technical breakthrough, but a redefinition of what it means to manage, lead, and build in the age of intelligent software.

Artificial General Intelligence: Definitional Horizon and Imminent Reality

Among all the predictions about the future of AI, none carries more weight—or more controversy—than the question of Artificial General

Intelligence (AGI). Often described as the moment when a machine can learn and perform any intellectual task that a human can, the moment of singularity, AGI is both a technical milestone and a cultural inflection point. Its arrival signals not just new capabilities, but a fundamental shift in the relationship between humans and machines.

Today's AI systems—no matter how advanced—are considered "narrow." They are trained to solve specific types of problems with tremendous efficiency, but they lack the generalized, flexible reasoning abilities that define human cognition. A large language model can summarize legal documents or generate code, but it doesn't truly "understand" the world. It lacks self-awareness, long-term memory, independent goals, or the capacity to transfer skills between unrelated domains.

AGI, by contrast, would have:

- Cross-domain competence: the ability to apply learning from one area to another with minimal retraining.
- Abstract reasoning: the capacity to understand, hypothesize, and model the world in complex, dynamic ways.
- Adaptability and initiative: the ability to take on new, unfamiliar tasks without human instruction.
- Meta-learning: the ability to reflect on its own learning and improve its problem-solving strategies over time.

These capabilities are not entirely theoretical. With the rise of increasingly large, multimodal models (trained on text, images, code, audio, and video) and emerging agentic systems capable of planning and goal-setting, we are edging closer to a practical realization of AGI—even if we don't yet have unanimous agreement on the precise criteria.

In fact, we predict that AGI will likely be achieved within the next 3 to 5 years. This forecast is not solely based on raw model size or compute acceleration—although both continue to grow exponentially. Rather, it reflects the convergence of multiple advancements:

- Multimodal fusion: integrating multiple types of input and reasoning together (text, vision, sound, etc.)
- Emergent agentic behaviors: AI agents that initiate, delegate, and self-improve without supervision
- Dynamic memory architectures: enabling models to retain, update, and recall past interactions across long time horizons
- Cognitive scaffolding frameworks: such as AutoGPT, ReAct, and Toolformer, which enhance reasoning with memory, tools, and feedback

What tempers our timeline is not technical feasibility alone—but the lack of a shared, rigorous definition of AGI. What constitutes "general" intelligence? Is it passing a comprehensive battery of tasks across disciplines? Matching the performance of a human across multiple jobs? Demonstrating sentient-like awareness or ethical reasoning? Until the industry, governments, and research institutions converge on a clear benchmark, the term itself remains fluid—more horizon than destination. Perhaps now is a good time to jump back to Chapter 3 to revisit the Turing test.

Still, we believe the defining threshold for AGI will emerge not just from academic theory, but from business practice. The moment when an AI system can operate across departments, initiate business improvements, learn from results, and reason about its own performance—without human configuration or retraining—that moment will mark a functional, if not philosophical, definition of general intelligence.

And platforms that serve as the operational foundation for such intelligence—such as the Intelligent Business Management Platform™ (IBMP)—will be the proving grounds. In these platforms, AGI won't arrive with a declaration or headline. It will arrive gradually, then all at once—as AI Tasks become indistinguishable from strategic decision-makers and as businesses begin to scale not just through capital or labor, but through the intelligence they've deployed.

In short, AGI is not a mythic endpoint—it is an evolving capability, getting closer every day. And the leaders who prepare for it now, with principled architecture and ethical foresight, will be the ones who shape its reality.

Geopolitical and Military Tensions in the Age of Advanced AI

As artificial intelligence advances from narrow utility to strategic infrastructure, it is not just reshaping industries—it is redrawing the boundaries of geopolitical influence. In *The Age of AI: And Our Human Future*, Henry Kissinger, Eric Schmidt, and Daniel Huttenlocher argue that AI will alter the fundamental calculus of national power, diplomacy, and warfare— redefining what it means to lead in the 21st century. Unlike past waves of technological disruption, the AI era is not additive. It is transformative. And that transformation is taking place on a global stage.

One of the most profound implications of AI's rise is its role in national security. Countries are racing not only to develop advanced AI systems but to dominate the data, hardware, and compute infrastructure that underpins them. This competition is no longer confined to economic or technological spheres—it has become a matter of national defense.

As Schmidt and Kissinger note, military doctrines are being rewritten to account for AI-driven surveillance, autonomous weaponry, cyberwarfare, and real-time decision support. Intelligence agencies are using AI to model adversary behavior and conduct influence operations. Autonomous drones and robotic systems are being tested for reconnaissance and combat missions. And battlefield strategy itself is being augmented by real-time analytics—where decisions must be made faster than human cognition allows.

This rapid militarization of AI poses unprecedented challenges:

- Accountability in autonomous systems: If a machine fires the first shot or misidentifies a target, who bears the responsibility? Traditional rules of engagement struggle to apply.
- AI escalation dynamics: As machines make faster decisions, the window for human diplomacy shrinks. An AI system trained for strategic advantage may unintentionally trigger conflict through misaligned incentives or opaque reasoning.
- Asymmetric capabilities: AI lowers the barrier to entry for non-state actors. With commercial models accessible worldwide, terrorist groups and rogue states can deploy powerful tools without traditional military infrastructure.
- Data sovereignty and digital borders: Nations are increasingly treating data as a strategic asset, enacting regulations that restrict AI training across borders and intensifying global fragmentation of the internet.

What Schmidt and Kissinger emphasize most is the dilemma of comprehension. The speed and complexity of advanced AI systems will soon exceed human ability to interpret or audit them. This creates a dangerous mismatch: geopolitical actors relying on systems they cannot fully control or explain, with implications they cannot fully foresee. In this environment, strategic clarity becomes existential.

The path forward, according to the authors, requires a global commitment to governance, ethics, and transparency. But that is easier said than done. While some nations call for multilateral AI safety standards, others prioritize dominance over diplomacy. This dissonance raises the specter of a new kind of arms race—one not marked by missiles, but by models.

As businesses and governments increasingly adopt AI for critical infrastructure, these risks will not remain abstract. They will be embedded in cloud platforms, transportation systems, financial markets, and supply chains. And as AI becomes integrated into military and commercial systems alike, the line between national defense and enterprise deployment will continue to blur.

It is in this context that responsible innovation becomes paramount. Platforms, while designed for civilian enterprise, must operate within a global framework that acknowledges the dual-use nature of AI. Intelligence, once deployed at scale, is not neutral. It carries implications far beyond its original use case.

In this new geopolitical reality, leadership in AI is not just about algorithms or infrastructure. It is about values—about ensuring that the systems we build do not just serve power, but preserve peace.

The Rise of AI-Native Business Models

In the 2010s, the concept of being "cloud-native" reshaped how companies were born. Startups no longer needed to invest in physical servers or build custom infrastructure from scratch. With AWS, Azure, and Google Cloud, they could scale globally in days. This shift fundamentally altered business velocity, cost structures, and investor expectations. Today, we are witnessing a similar—but more profound—transition: the rise of *AI-native* businesses.

AI-native companies will not simply use AI—they will be architected around it. Their operational DNA will assume AI is not an enhancement but a baseline. These organizations are not retrofitting legacy systems or layering generative tools onto traditional workflows. Instead, they are designed from the ground up with artificial intelligence as the central nervous system.

Key Characteristics of AI-Native Businesses

The blueprint for an AI-native business departs dramatically from conventional models. Its most defining features include:

- AI-driven onboarding, support, and training: New users will be welcomed, trained, and supported not by manuals or support reps, but by intelligent agents. These agents will guide users through product adoption, answer questions contextually, and provide personalized learning experiences.
- Task-based revenue models: Rather than offering flat software licenses or consulting packages, AI-native firms will monetize modular *Tasks*—discrete, intelligent services that businesses can deploy on demand. Pricing will be based on outcomes, usage volume, or strategic value, not seat counts.
- Continuous optimization through autonomous analytics: These businesses will not wait for quarterly reviews or manual audits. Embedded AI agents will monitor operational performance in real time, making micro-adjustments to workflows, marketing strategies, inventory levels, and customer engagement based on live data.

- Minimal reliance on human-led administration: From payroll to compliance to procurement, the "back office" will largely be executed by AI. Human operators will be system architects and ethical overseers, not task executors. Teams will be smaller, more technical, and more focused on managing intelligence rather than managing people.

In many ways, this shift echoes the industrial revolutions of the past. Just as mechanization reduced the need for manual labor in factories, AI will reduce the need for manual process management in offices. But unlike the past, the tools of this revolution are not machines of muscle—they are machines of thought.

One of the clearest benefits of next-generation AI, and the AI native business model, is the ability to continuously adapt to new information. Dynamic pricing—already used by companies like Amazon and Uber—will become far more granular and autonomous. AI systems will evaluate real-time supply chain data, customer behavior, competitor activity, and macroeconomic signals to make pricing decisions in seconds, not weeks.

Beyond pricing, we will see the rise of autonomous decision systems that can:

- Adjust marketing spend by channel in real time

- Allocate human resources based on predicted workloads

- Trigger product restocks based on consumption trends

- Evaluate partner relationships using dynamic trust scores

These systems will not replace human oversight, but they will evolve some of the roles of leadership—shifting from decision-making to decision-framing.

The Role of Intelligent Business Management Platforms™

As these new businesses emerge, they require a platform that reflects their native environment, such as the Intelligent Business Management Platform™.

AI-native startups and SMBs will adopt an IBMP solution not as an alternative to legacy systems, but as their default infrastructure. With limited resources, these businesses will rely on platforms like LIBBi™ to execute core functions without needing to hire full departments. A founder can launch a business with:

- A virtual sales agent handling outreach and qualification.
- An AI finance Task managing invoicing, billing, and reconciliations.
- A customer support assistant resolving tickets via chat.
- An operations dashboard powered by real-time AI insights.

This level of operational leverage was unimaginable just a few years ago. But now, the barrier to entry for intelligent execution is no longer capital—it is vision.

From "Hiring Staff" to "Activating Intelligence"

Perhaps the most striking cultural change of AI-native businesses will be how they approach growth. Traditional companies grow by hiring people to fill gaps in capacity. AI-native businesses grow by activating Tasks. Need to expand your customer support? Add a new language model. Want to analyze market trends? Spin up a forecasting agent. Looking to build an onboarding system? Deploy a training Task and monitor performance in real time.

In this world, headcount is no longer the sole indicator of organizational scale. Instead, businesses will be measured by how effectively they orchestrate intelligence—how agilely they can reconfigure workflows and how efficiently they can turn ideas into execution.

Implications for Leadership and Innovation

This shift will not only affect how businesses operate—it will change what leadership looks like. Founders and executives must become fluent not just in management, but in Task design, data strategy, and ethical oversight. They will need to understand how to direct AI without micromanaging it, how to extract insight without violating privacy, and how to scale without losing human intuition.

Furthermore, the rise of AI-native businesses will challenge regulatory frameworks, labor models, and corporate norms. Governments will need to consider how to define employment, taxation, and IP ownership in firms that operate with minimal human labor. Investors will need new metrics to value companies whose cost structures and team dynamics diverge radically from tradition.

Infrastructure Arms Race: The Backbone of AI Advancement

As the capabilities of artificial intelligence surge forward, a parallel—but often overlooked—race is underway: the race to build and control the infrastructure that powers it. From high-performance compute clusters and advanced semiconductor fabrication to fiber-optic networks, cloud data centers, and energy grids, the next era of AI dominance will be determined not only by algorithms, but by infrastructure.

Government Investment: Strategic Necessity

Across the globe, governments are beginning to understand that leadership in AI is not solely a matter of research and regulation—it's a matter of infrastructure sovereignty. The United States, in particular, has significantly increased funding for AI-related hardware and network development through agencies like the Department of Energy (DOE), the Department of Defense (DoD), and the National Science Foundation (NSF). These investments are not just academic—they are strategic.

For example, the CHIPS and Science Act of 2022 allocated over $52 billion in subsidies and incentives for semiconductor research and manufacturing on U.S. soil. While the legislation's intent was to reduce dependence on foreign chipmakers—especially those based in Taiwan—it also signaled a broader recognition: AI innovation depends on physical computing power. And whoever controls that power controls the pace of progress.

Similarly, the U.S. Department of Defense has launched initiatives such as the Joint Artificial Intelligence Center (JAIC) and Project Maven to apply AI in defense operations, cybersecurity, and logistics. These projects require not only data science talent but enormous computational backbones, leading to new public-private partnerships aimed at scaling secure, high-availability compute resources.

Internationally, countries like China, the UK, France, and the United Arab Emirates are investing heavily in sovereign AI cloud services, domestic GPU farms, and next-gen networking technologies. This is not just an economic effort—it is geopolitical positioning.

Corporate Investments: Data Centers, Energy, and Bandwidth

In the corporate world, AI leaders like Microsoft, Google, Amazon, Meta, and NVIDIA are pouring billions into the infrastructure behind AI—not just the models themselves. Microsoft, for instance, has partnered with OpenAI while simultaneously expanding Azure data centers globally to serve high-demand AI workloads. In 2023 alone, Microsoft announced investments in additional U.S.-based AI data centers in Iowa, Georgia, and Texas, aiming to make Azure the dominant platform for enterprise-scale model deployment.

Google, meanwhile, continues to scale its Tensor Processing Units (TPUs) and edge AI hardware while investing in subsea cables and next-gen internet routing to ensure low-latency, high-throughput access to its models. Meta has announced plans to refocus much of its infrastructure spending from the metaverse to AI compute, dedicating tens of billions to build out GPU farms optimized for LLM training and inference.

Behind the scenes, chipmaker NVIDIA is enabling much of this growth. Its H100 and A100 chips are the new gold standard for deep learning infrastructure. Demand has far outstripped supply, leading companies and even nations to treat access to NVIDIA's chips as a strategic resource.

But hardware is only part of the story.

AI workloads—especially training large language models and generative systems—consume enormous amounts of energy and connectivity bandwidth. A single training run for a frontier LLM like GPT-4 is estimated to use enough electricity to power hundreds of U.S. homes for a year. As a result, companies are racing to co-locate data centers near renewable energy sources, sign long-term power agreements with utilities, and build energy-efficient liquid-cooled server farms.

In addition to compute and power, networking infrastructure is critical. AI-native applications require low-latency internet access and real-time synchronization across devices and users. Cloudflare, Akamai, and other edge computing providers are expanding distributed networks to support inference at scale, reducing lag and ensuring secure delivery.

Challenges on the Horizon

This infrastructure boom, however, is not without challenges. As demand outpaces supply in areas like GPUs, energy, and fiber-optic bandwidth, we may see bottlenecks that slow innovation or shift competitive advantage toward nations and companies with more secure supply chains. Environmental impact is another growing concern, as AI's energy usage becomes a larger slice of global consumption. Without sustainable practices, the ecological footprint of the AI revolution could become a liability.

The Infrastructure Future of IBMPs

For Intelligent Business Management Platforms™ solutions like LIBBi, this infrastructure conversation is not theoretical—it is operational. As AI Tasks become more embedded in the daily functioning of businesses, they will rely on real-time access to high-performance models, reliable connectivity, and secure data hosting. The success of IBMPs will, in many ways, hinge on how well they can scale compute and bandwidth without sacrificing latency or privacy.

Emerging solutions like distributed inference, task-specific fine-tuning, and on-device processing will help reduce infrastructure strain and improve performance. Still, the future of intelligent business remains intertwined with the broader infrastructure arms race.

AI is no longer just a software revolution—it is an infrastructure revolution. Those who control the physical, electrical, and computational scaffolding of artificial intelligence will control the speed, shape, and spread of its impact. For governments, this is a matter of security. For corporations, it is a matter of survival. For the rest of us, it is the unseen but essential foundation of the world we are building.

Ubiquitous Adoption: AI Becomes Standard Operating Procedure

If the last decade was defined by AI experimentation, the next five years will mark the transition to AI ubiquity. Just as email, cloud computing, and CRM systems eventually became baseline business requirements—not optional innovations—so too will artificial intelligence become foundational to operations, decision-making, and growth. AI is moving from the edge to the core of business—and from novelty to necessity.

From Optional Add-On to Operational Expectation

A major inflection point is already underway. As of 2024, more than 77% of organizations globally have reported some form of AI adoption in at least one business function, according to McKinsey's Global AI Survey. But in practice, most of these deployments remain isolated—siloed tools for marketing automation, chatbots, or document summarization. The result is a landscape of fragmented adoption: AI is present, but its impact is often inconsistent or superficial.

That landscape is changing rapidly.

Driven by pressure to cut costs, increase agility, and improve decision speed, businesses of all sizes are recognizing that piecemeal AI doesn't scale. Maintaining a dozen disconnected AI tools—each with separate integrations, data silos, and usage patterns—is costly, inefficient, and insecure. The next phase of AI adoption is marked by consolidation: businesses are looking for unified platforms that embed intelligence across the entire operation.

This realization is leading to the rise of comprehensive systems, where AI is no longer a tool *used by* business software, but the foundation of the business software itself.

Solutions like the Intelligent Business Management Platform™ are a clear embodiment of this future. Rather than relying on legacy platforms with retrofitted AI plug-ins, an IBMP solution is built from the ground up with AI as their operating system. These platforms integrate data, processes, interfaces, and AI agents in a seamless, secure architecture—eliminating the need for costly integrations and manual oversight.

Businesses are increasingly adopting IBMPs because they offer:

- Task-based execution: Rather than jumping between SaaS tools, users simply ask for an outcome and AI Tasks execute it—whether it's scheduling a meeting, onboarding a client, or generating financial reports.
- Natural-language interfaces: AI-driven chat replaces clunky dashboards, allowing employees to interact with complex systems as easily as they'd use a messaging app.
- End-to-end integration: Sales, finance, HR, marketing, and support all operate from a shared, AI-enhanced environment, enabling cross-functional visibility and efficiency.

- Scalable intelligence: AI capabilities can be expanded on demand—from predictive analytics to generative design—without adding new vendors or licenses.

As adoption increases, businesses are also discovering that AI maturity brings network effects. Each new Task executed, each data set integrated, each decision enhanced improves the overall system—making IBMPs smarter, faster, and more valuable over time.

Small Businesses, Big Gains

One of the most striking trends in this shift is the rapid acceleration of AI adoption among small and mid-sized businesses (SMBs). Historically, these organizations have been slow to adopt enterprise technology due to cost and complexity. But IBMPs—many of which offer AI Tasks through one-click activation and transparent billing—are democratizing access to enterprise-grade AI.

Instead of hiring a full operations team or managing a stack of software subscriptions, a small business can launch a fully intelligent back-office in minutes. The result is a flattening of traditional advantages: AI is leveling the playing field, giving lean teams the power to act with enterprise precision.

A Future Without the AI Tab

Within five years, AI will likely be as invisible—and as essential—as electricity in the office. Businesses won't talk about "using AI" the same way they no longer talk about "using the internet." The tools, insights, and automation AI provides will be baked into the workflow, not bolted on.

The question facing most businesses is no longer whether to adopt AI—but how to adopt it effectively. In the coming wave, those who integrate AI deeply into their operations will gain agility, insight, and scalability that others cannot match. As with cloud computing a decade ago, the shift won't be universal overnight—but it will be inevitable.

Final Thoughts: From Forecast to Frontline

In 1876, Alexander Graham Bell stood in a modest Boston workshop and made history with a simple sentence: *"Mr. Watson, come here, I want to see you."* The telephone had been born—not fully formed, not fully understood, but unmistakably revolutionary. Most dismissed it as a novelty. Western Union famously turned down the opportunity to buy the telephone patent for $100,000, calling it a toy. Yet within a few decades, the telephone had redefined business, communication, and global connection.

Artificial intelligence today is having its "Bell moment." It has arrived—not as a toy, but as a tool that will reshape how we work, build, govern, and compete. What remains uncertain is not *whether* AI will be adopted universally, but *how well* it will be integrated—and by whom. Just like the telephone, early movers who understand the strategic value of this shift will gain a permanent advantage.

The chapters in Part II have looked forward, outlining a near future defined by fully autonomous agents, artificial general intelligence, geopolitical stakes, and AI-native operational models. These developments are not science fiction—they are unfolding now. And they are reshaping the business landscape with breathtaking speed.

But forecasting the future is not the same as preparing for it. That's where we go next.

Part III: Cutting Through the Noise.

In Chapter 6, we shift from possibility to practice. You'll learn how to evaluate your business for AI readiness, prioritize the right AI tasks, and implement solutions using modern platforms. No matter your industry or team size, the AI era has begun. And it's time to make it real, in your business, today.

Chapter 6: Cutting Through the Noise and Finding Simplicity

In the late 1990s, Kodak stood at the summit of its industry. Its name was shorthand for photography itself. Its distribution network spanned the globe. Its market dominance felt absolute.

And yet, within Kodak's own labs, a team of engineers had already built the future: one of the first working digital cameras. It wasn't a rough prototype. It was real. It worked. But it never made it to market.

Leadership buried it.

Why? Because Kodak's core business was built around film. The revenue, the supply chain, the infrastructure—it all depended on a model that digital photography would disrupt. So rather than shift, they protected the system they knew.

The result is now a business school cliché: while Kodak stalled, companies like Canon, Nikon, and eventually Apple and Samsung redefined photography. Kodak, with all its brand equity and talent, missed the moment. Not because they didn't see it—but because they couldn't cut through the complexity of their own success to act on it.

AI presents a similar inflection point for today's businesses.

In the past five chapters, we've moved from the roots of artificial intelligence to its current reality: large language models, generative tools, and intelligent platforms now shaping how modern businesses think, decide, and operate. Chapter 5 offered a glimpse into what's coming next—agentic systems, AI-native organizations, and an ecosystem that will reward adaptability over scale, and simplicity over legacy.

Now, in Chapter 6, we return to the present moment—with urgency and with clarity.

This chapter isn't about hype. It's about what's actually working. It's about cutting through saturated markets, bloated feature sets, and marketing noise to focus on solutions that help businesses move forward—especially those without the luxury of multi-year digital transformation budgets.

Here, we introduce the concept of AI Tasks—tools designed to make adoption frictionless and functionality intuitive. We argue that consumer-grade simplicity must now be the standard for enterprise-grade intelligence. And we explore what it means to run a business on AI without needing to "learn AI" at all.

Because if Kodak taught us anything, it's this: complexity isn't strength. Clarity is.

And in this new era, success will belong to the businesses that can cut through the noise—and build what's next. Simply.

The Illusion of AI Saturation

To the casual observer, the market feels "full." Every productivity tool, CRM, scheduling platform, and design app now claims some form of AI integration. LinkedIn ads pitch "AI for sales teams" not to mention the constant barrage of LinkedIn messages from consultants who can help you adopt some AI tool. YouTube pre-rolls show AI writing copy or doing your taxes. App marketplaces are flooded with thousands of "AI-enhanced" offerings.

We have seen this first-hand in our journey building InChannel AI. We have referred to InChannel AI as among the first businesses to operate on AI. What we really mean is that we have used AI tools and Tasks to support our business almost from the start. In the early days, this reliance on AI tools was both a necessity and a way for us to dig deep on the current state of the industry. Over time we explored the 100,000+ AI tools and Tasks that existed in the current market at that time and honed our list. Today, we rely almost exclusively on LIBBi and the AI Tasks that exist in its marketplace, many created by third-party developers who participate in the LIBBi Task Workspace program. As a business operating on AI, we have certainly come to understand the power and the illusion of saturation, what works and what does little or nothing productive.

But behind the curtain, many of these platforms use AI only in name. At most, they've added a chatbot or an LLM wrapper to an otherwise traditional architecture. In many cases, these tools are siloed, shallow, or overly specific—great for a single task, but incapable of scaling across a business.

And what's worse: they rarely talk to each other.

Businesses today are trapped in an exhausting loop—adopting one tool for project management, another for contracts, a third for invoicing, a fourth for accessing some needed industry data like insurance pricing, and yet another for marketing. Each requires its own subscription, data upload, security compliance, onboarding, and training. Each has its own interface, dashboards, and logic. Each demands time, configuration, and maintenance. And still, they often fail to connect meaningfully with one another.

So instead of operating a business, teams spend their time stitching one app to another—copying data, navigating integration breakdowns, juggling logins, and reformatting reports just to keep operations moving forward.

The result is not empowerment. It's fragmentation.

The true saturation isn't in capability—it's in confusion. Most businesses are not suffering from a lack of options. They're suffering from too many—each solving part of the problem, while quietly creating others. That's not simplicity. That's complexity disguised as innovation.

The Power of Being Early

The most transformative business outcomes rarely happen when a technology is mature and widely adopted. They happen at inflection points—when a business adopts earlier than the rest, learns faster, and builds culture around it before the competition even notices.

Just as the early adopters of cloud infrastructure in the 2010s outpaced their competitors in scale and cost, the businesses that become AI-native first will dominate their verticals in the years ahead.

This doesn't mean building your own models or hiring a team of data scientists. It means adopting tools that are designed around AI from the start—platforms where intelligence isn't an accessory, but a core design principle.

Knowing What to Look For: Five Characteristics of AI-Centric Platforms

To separate signal from noise, business leaders must learn to recognize what real, AI-first solutions look like. We've identified five key characteristics that define truly AI-native platforms—some framed by what they include, and others by what they deliberately reject.

1.   AI is Embedded Throughout the Platform

In an AI-centric solution, intelligence is not bolted on—it's built in. You'll see AI woven into the user interface (often chat- or voice-driven), the core logic, the analytics engine, and the support functions. These platforms don't just add AI; they are designed to work *through* it. If the experience starts and ends with clicking buttons in a dashboard, it's likely not AI-native.

2.   AI Is Not a Wrapper or Add-On

Be cautious of tools that rely solely on plugging ChatGPT into an existing workflow or launching with a shiny "AI Assistant" button. These are often wrappers—interfaces placed on top of legacy software that was never intended to be intelligent. True AI platforms avoid this altogether. Their architecture is designed from the ground up with AI as the operating principle—not an enhancement.

3. Rapid Integration of New AI Tasks and Tools

AI-first systems don't require a software engineer to add capabilities. They're built to expand dynamically—whether through activating new AI Tasks, integrating other models or third-party tools, or embedding external LLMs. If adding functionality requires complex code or vendor support, it's not future-proof. AI-centric platforms allow users to grow their intelligence stack with just a few clicks.

4. Dynamic, Auto-Updating Web Interfaces

Most platforms treat websites and customer portals as static objects. AI-first platforms treat them as living systems. A user-facing interface should update dynamically—reflecting changes to tasks, business status, or new offerings in real time. If it requires a developer to publish a change or a marketing team to update a form, it isn't truly intelligent.

5. Centralized, Siloed, and Accessible Business Data

At the heart of any AI platform is data—and how it's structured. AI-native platforms store all user data in a centralized, vectorized format, siloed for security and assigned to that user alone. That data is then made available to all Tasks and analysis tools across the platform. This eliminates redundant uploads, prevents data leaks, and powers cross-functional intelligence without the need for custom integrations.

When a platform meets all five of these characteristics, it is not just AI-compatible—it is AI-native. And in an era of widespread noise, that distinction is everything.

Why Simplicity Is a Strategic Advantage

In the race to adopt AI, it's not just about who gets there first—it's about who can actually use it.

Speed matters. But clarity wins.

While early adopters gain an advantage by moving fast, the ones who sustain that lead are those who make adoption easy—for their teams, their customers, and their operations. In a landscape crowded with dashboards, APIs, and buzzwords, simplicity becomes more than a design preference. It becomes a strategic advantage–especially when the satisfaction of your customers is a premier concern.

Simplicity doesn't mean dumbing things down. It means removing friction. It means creating tools that can be used without an IT department, that fit naturally into daily workflows, and that feel less like "learning AI" and more like just doing your job—better. It means creating engaging and frictionless experiences for your customers, who access your products or services through your AI-native solution.

As we explored in Chapter 4, many legacy systems attempt to retrofit intelligence into infrastructure that was never meant to scale it. AI is slapped on as a widget, a button, or a wrapper. The result? Platforms that are technically powerful, but practically unusable. Teams spend more time configuring than executing. Even simple workflows—like client onboarding or internal reporting—require prompt engineering, dashboard gymnastics, or third-party consultants just to operate.

That's not intelligence. That's overhead.

The true strategic edge comes from platforms that make intelligence usable. AI should enhance your decisions without requiring you to become a data scientist. It should automate with precision, not overwhelm with options. And most importantly, it should scale without dragging complexity along with it.

In business, complexity often masquerades as capability. But in the era of AI, simplicity is what unlocks scale.

When systems are intuitive, adoption accelerates. When intelligence is embedded—not bolted on—your team moves faster, your data works harder, and your business becomes not just more efficient, but more agile. That's the new advantage.

And that's what simplicity, done right, delivers.

We learned this lesson firsthand.

Early in our launch of InChannel AI, we took on a client who was working to stand up a new platform—both as a learning opportunity and to generate some much-needed revenue. The contract involved integrating early features of what would eventually become our LIBBi platform: intelligent chat, a dynamic website, and a handful of AI-integrated tasks, at that time. We were also responsible for helping the firm promote its solution within the waste management industry.

But because our own platform was still in early development, we had to rely heavily on third-party tools—some that marketed themselves as AI-driven, and others that were more traditional SaaS. What started out as a practical necessity quickly became a masterclass in frustration.

We had to learn—and in some cases painfully reverse engineer—dashboard logic across five or more tools. Each platform had its own quirks: new interface, new terminology, new workflows, new integrations (or lack thereof), and the now infamous "secret option" that when unknowingly selected makes key things fail to work, like the ability to sign up a new customer. We spent days configuring email sequences in one app, only to struggle with how to link that data to CRM tags in another. We ran into tool limits, missing API connections, broken automations, and poorly documented "AI features" that were more hype than help.

At some point, it took longer to learn how to *use* the software than it would have to just *do* the work ourselves manually. And we suspect, if you've spent any time managing digital systems, you've had similar experiences. If not— we hope you're reading this early enough that adopting a true AI-first platform helps you avoid this entirely.

This is the reality for too many teams: they aren't underperforming because they lack ideas, talent, or effort. They're underperforming because their systems are working *against* them. The technology that was meant to simplify operations has done the opposite—adding friction at every turn.

The truth is, most business users don't need another API, dashboard, or plugin. They need simplicity. They need a system that works the way they work—fluid, fast, and easy to understand. A system that delivers results, not just features. And the good news is that the power of AI, properly deployed, can make every business solution not only intelligent, but intuitive and simple.

After all, AI is only useful if it's used. And it's only used if it's usable.

One-Click Activation – The Dream: From Integration Nightmare to Invisible Intelligence

For decades, the dream of seamless integration has loomed just out of reach—a future where third-party tools, intelligent workflows, and bespoke automations could be activated instantly within a business's existing architecture. No long discovery calls. No outside consultants. No multi-month IT deployment plan. Just one click. It has always seemed like a reasonable goal in theory. In practice, it's been nearly impossible to achieve.

The core challenge is that most business platforms—especially the large, legacy systems like Salesforce, Odoo, Accumatica, or NetSuite—were never designed for this level of simplicity. Their architectures are modular but rigid. Adding functionality often means modifying schemas, configuring workflows, integrating APIs, and granting access credentials across systems with different rules, structures, and data formats. Each new app, extension, or "plugin" introduces a cascade of hidden dependencies. And once something breaks, the complexity reveals itself: configuration conflicts, update mismatches, misaligned permissions, missing context. The vision of one-click integration is buried under technical debt.

Even the platforms that promised modularity have consistently failed to deliver true plug-and-play extensibility. CRMs and ERPs often require a network of consultants, certified implementers, or agency partners to "make it all work." Business leaders must navigate internal IT approvals, security audits, and the dreaded learning curve of a new interface. The time and cost involved in standing up a new workflow are sometimes greater than the problem the workflow was meant to solve.

The result is inertia. Instead of agile operations, businesses are locked into static systems. Instead of innovation, they adapt themselves to the limitations of their tools.

It's no surprise, then, that the idea of *true* one-click integration—especially for complex, intelligent tasks—has remained aspirational.

Yet we have seen it work in other domains.

Take, for example, the now-famous Amazon Dash button. Introduced in 2015, the Dash was a small wireless device that could be stuck to a washing machine, refrigerator, or shelf. One press of the button would automatically reorder household products—detergent, diapers, coffee—with no need to open a laptop, check inventory, or confirm a shipping address. It was intelligent execution hidden inside an elegant form. You pressed a button. The system took care of the rest.

It was a simple act. But behind that simplicity was an intricate cascade: user authentication, inventory tracking, preference recall, address verification, payment processing, and shipment routing. All invisible to the user. That's the essence of what today's AI can—and should—enable for business.

This is what the one-click Task model aspires to achieve. Intelligence delivering simplicity.

As a case study, we have worked hard to deliver on this promise in building our LIBBi solution. And, its fair to say, it has been a challenge, requiring us to build every element of the system's architecture with this one-click simplicity in mind. We're proud to have successfully introduced the concept of the one-click task—a paradigm shift in how business automation is delivered. Rather than requiring integrations, scripting, or custom workflows, a one-click task is exactly what it sounds like: a business function (an AI Task) any business can implement in its system instantly, with one click.

We've gone further and implemented the functionality within a chat, allowing a user to simply write or speak what they want to accomplish with natural language. LIBBi identifies the task, understands the goal, recommends the AI Task, and the user can activate it with one click. Once activated, the Task accesses the appropriate data, executes the workflow, and confirms the result—all within the same conversational flow. There's no toggling between apps, no uploading CSV files, no watching tutorials. To the business operator, it feels like a conversation with an associate who already understands the context, the systems, and the objective.

But make no mistake: behind that single click is an orchestration engine. It parses input, matches it to structured agents, dynamically formats prompts, checks access permissions, applies business rules, syncs across tools, and maintains logs. It's like the analogy of a graceful duck, we see it elegantly and effortlessly moving across the pond but, under the water, it's paddling hard and in a way honed by ducks over generations.

In the end, that's the power of well-designed intelligence: it lets the complexity run deep so the experience can remain simple. The best AI tools won't require a user manual, a week of training, or a consultant to interpret them. They'll just work—quietly, reliably, and in context. Simplicity, when done right, isn't the absence of sophistication. It's the deliberate decision to let the machinery serve the moment, not dominate it. In a world flooded with features and overwhelmed by choice, the businesses that win won't be the ones with the flashiest tools—they'll be the ones whose systems are so intuitive, their teams hardly notice the AI is there at all. That's not a constraint. It's the benchmark. Simplicity isn't just good design—it's strategic advantage.

Consumer-Grade Usability, Enterprise-Grade Intelligence

There's a reason tools like the iPhone, Slack, and Canva achieved widespread adoption—particularly in domains previously dominated by complex, overengineered software. These products weren't just functional; they were intuitive. They didn't require manuals, onboarding sessions, or IT support. They simply worked. And users—from small business owners to enterprise teams—gravitated toward them because of it.

They delivered consumer-grade usability alongside enterprise-grade capability, creating a new benchmark for what modern software should feel like: powerful, yet effortless.

As artificial intelligence becomes more deeply embedded in business software, this pairing is no longer aspirational. It is essential.

But what exactly does *consumer-grade usability* mean in the context of enterprise software?

At its core, it means designing tools for professionals with the same standards of ease, immediacy, and elegance that consumers expect in personal apps. Business tools should be as satisfying and seamless to use as the ones we use at home. This includes:

1.   Minimal Cognitive Load

The system anticipates user intent, guiding them through intuitive workflows without requiring them to remember commands, toggle hidden settings, or reference help documentation. Good design reduces thinking, not increases it.

2.	Natural Language Interaction

Users engage through chat, speech, or simplified visual inputs—no coding, scripting, or database querying required. Communication becomes human, not mechanical.

3.	No Technical Translation Layer

Users should not be forced to "speak software" to use software. They should not need to understand APIs, set up webhooks, or configure third-party integrations just to automate routine tasks.

4.	Instant Feedback and Visible Results

When users take action, results are immediate and visible. Changes apply in real time. Successes are acknowledged, and errors are caught early. The interface feels responsive and conversational.

5.	Customization Without Complexity

Users can personalize outputs and experiences—be it reports, messages, or dashboards—without needing a developer. Pre-built structures provide smart defaults with easy adjustment points.

Slack is a classic case study. While technically a messaging platform, it supports file sharing, calls, custom notifications, integrations, and even automation—all within an interface simple enough to use from day one. It doesn't feel like a business tool; it feels like a conversation. Users don't need training to use it. They just do.

Canva transformed the design process in much the same way. Where tools like Adobe Photoshop required months of training and creative expertise, and arguably offered more power to a user, Canva made high-quality design accessible to anyone. Drag-and-drop components, smart templates, and AI-powered suggestions turned the once-daunting task of building presentations or marketing collateral into a fluid, even fun experience.

And of course, the iPhone remains the gold standard for marrying complexity with simplicity. Its internal architecture runs some of the most advanced consumer hardware ever made—yet users never have to think about it. From camera enhancements to biometric security, the intelligence is deeply embedded, but always in the background.

This is the challenge for AI in business: to mirror the elegance and approachability of consumer apps while delivering the scale, security, and sophistication that enterprises demand. The true breakthrough in AI will not come from building smarter models—it will come from making those models disappear into seamless experiences.

In this context, the metric for success shifts:

- Can users get results without reading a manual?

- Can they initiate AI-powered workflows with natural language?

- Can they make meaningful changes without technical help?

- Can they trust the system without needing to understand how it works?

If the answer is yes, then the platform has achieved something extraordinary: it has made intelligence usable.

Because ultimately, the tools that win are not just those that *can* do more—but those that demand less of the user to do it.

Should AI Be Invisible?

This is more than a usability feature. It's a philosophical position.

In an age of overwhelming interfaces, vendor sprawl, and configuration fatigue, simplicity becomes a form of strategic advantage. Today's most effective tools are not those that overwhelm with options or flaunt their intelligence—they're the ones that quietly do the job and get out of the way. In short: tools that are truly intelligent don't just perform—they disappear. They do the work, not demand it.

For decades, the enterprise software world has normalized complexity. Dashboards became deeper. Menus grew longer. APIs multiplied. Every new system brought more training sessions, more specialist certifications, more friction. Businesses were conditioned to expect that intelligence would come at the cost of usability—and that real power meant real overhead.

But what we're learning now is that the most impactful systems are those that hide their complexity behind the cleanest user experiences. They don't ask the user to understand how they work—they just work.

This idea—that the smartest technology should be invisible—has precedent in other transformative products. Take, for instance, the Nest Learning Thermostat.

When Nest launched in 2011, the home thermostat was a device most people barely noticed, let alone appreciated. It was functional but opaque. Programming it required navigating nested buttons and arcane interfaces— so most people simply didn't. They adjusted it manually or left it running inefficiently. Smart home products existed, but they were clunky and largely reserved for the tech-savvy.

Nest changed that—not by adding more features, but by making its intelligence disappear into the background.

The Nest thermostat didn't just let you control your home's temperature from your phone. It learned your habits. It noticed when you left the house. It adjusted the climate for energy savings while you were away, and warmed things up just before you returned. It used motion sensors, time-based algorithms, and data from other users to optimize performance. But the magic was that you never had to think about it. You didn't need to configure a complex automation schedule. You didn't need to set up "rules." You just turned the dial a few times during your first week, and after that—it quietly handled the rest.

People raved about Nest not because it explained what it was doing—but because it no longer needed to. The intelligence was embedded. The experience was seamless. And it was, in a very real sense, *invisible.*

This is the promise of AI in business software: not that it will dazzle users with complexity, but that it will remove it entirely.

The rise of one-click Tasks represents this turning point. They are not just about convenience or novelty. They're about redefining how intelligence is delivered—and how work gets done.

In a world where most tools still require configuration, scripting, or layered integrations, the one-click task says: *what if you didn't have to touch any of that?* What if an intelligent agent could read your request, understand your context, access your data, and execute the right steps—all before you even switch tabs?

•	Instead of navigating a 12-step onboarding flow, a user types "Add a new team member," and the system configures permissions, sends the welcome email, schedules onboarding, and logs the action.

•	Instead of toggling between scheduling, marketing, and analytics tools, a business owner types, "Launch a 3-day promo campaign," and the system builds it end-to-end.

This isn't just productivity. It's philosophy in action.

Because when AI works this way, it doesn't feel like AI. It feels like progress.

And if the user doesn't notice how smart the system is—only how effective it is—then that may be the highest compliment we can pay the future of intelligent software.

Final Thoughts: From Complexity to Clarity

As we move into an era where every business will use AI, the winners won't be those with the most tools—but those with the fewest points of friction. They'll be the companies with the clearest execution, the smoothest workflows, and the shortest distance between intention and result. In this new landscape, clarity isn't a byproduct of good design—it's the strategy itself.

This chapter has challenged the assumption that intelligence must come with overhead. We've examined the market's saturation of disconnected tools, exposed the myth of "AI-enhanced" platforms that do little more than bolt on a chatbot, and introduced the paradigm shift made possible by one-click tasks and invisible orchestration.

The message is clear: simplicity is not weakness. It's a form of power.

The businesses that thrive in this new era will be those that deploy intelligence without apparent complexity. Who solve real problems, not by assembling software pieces, but by activating purpose-built solutions that "just work." Because the future of AI isn't about showing how smart your tools are—it's about how little your people have to think about them.

But behind every seamless user experience is something else entirely: an architecture. A developer ecosystem. A platform built not only to support automation, but to scale it across tasks, teams, and time zones. That's where we're headed next.

In Chapter 7, we move from the front-end user experience to the systems and ecosystems that power it. We'll explore how modern platforms are designed around intelligent orchestration and how new standards in developer monetization and task portability are enabling a generation of builders to transform business at scale.

Chapter 7: Powered by Freelance — Building the AI Task Universe

In the summer of 2008, something quiet but foundational changed in the way technology was built and delivered. Apple opened the App Store. It launched with just 500 apps. Within a year, there were 50,000. Today, there are over two million.

But the real breakthrough wasn't in the software itself—it was in the shift of who was allowed to build.

The App Store didn't scale because Apple had more engineers. It scaled because it invited everyone else in: developers working from coffee shops, students in dorm rooms, freelancers in basements. Apple provided the infrastructure, the rails, and the marketplace. The developers brought the creativity. The result wasn't just convenience—it was the first truly decentralized innovation ecosystem built for scale.

And now, AI is following the same pattern.

For years, AI development was centralized—massive models, hosted by a few dominant players, offered through narrow APIs or rigid platforms. The tools were powerful, but inaccessible. Tailored use cases were hard to find. Distribution was unclear. For most businesses, the promise of intelligent software felt just out of reach.

That's changing.

As explored in Chapters 5 and 6, we're living through a shift not just in technology—but in how intelligence is delivered. AI is moving from generalized platforms to modular solutions. From abstract capabilities to real-world tasks. From dashboards to natural language. And underneath all of it, a new layer of builders is emerging: freelance AI developers.

These aren't enterprise architects building from the top down. They're specialists building from the middle out—solving one business problem at a time. They're crafting AI-powered Tasks that summarize contracts, route forms, detect sales signals, or flag billing anomalies. Small actions. Big impact. Just like those early App Store developers, they're creating the long tail of functionality—the things that major platforms overlook, but businesses need every day.

This chapter is about the infrastructure behind the interface.

We'll look at how these AI Tasks are created, where they live, and how they scale. We'll examine the practical barriers—distribution, monetization, data access, and integration—and how new platform architectures are beginning to resolve them. We'll explore:

- How freelance development is redefining innovation in AI

- Why most businesses still struggle with integration—and what comes next

- How Intelligent Business Management Platforms are creating space for builders

- The rise of AI-powered marketplaces and the emergence of on-demand Task economies

- And why modular, decentralized intelligence may prove to be the most scalable software model of the next decade

This isn't about apps anymore. It's about atomic actions—small, intelligent building blocks that can be combined, shared, and scaled across industries.

Welcome to the AI Task universe: a living, dynamic economy of modular intelligence—built by many, used by all, and quietly transforming how work gets done.

A New Age of Developer Empowerment—and the Freelance Economy Behind It

The rise of freelance AI development is not occurring in a vacuum—it's part of a much larger shift in how work is structured, monetized, and scaled.

Today, more than 70 million Americans participate in the freelance economy in some form, accounting for nearly 40% of the U.S. workforce. That figure is expected to exceed 50% within the next decade. The reasons are clear: flexibility, autonomy, and the ability to monetize specialized skills on demand. And this model doesn't just work—it scales.

Some of the most disruptive companies of the past two decades have grown by embracing this structure. Uber transformed transportation by treating cars and drivers as distributed infrastructure. Airbnb did the same with housing. Upwork and Fiverr built marketplaces that enabled independent professionals to deliver design, engineering, marketing, and business services—without joining a traditional company.

Upwork alone facilitated over $4 billion in freelance earnings last year, with more than 18 million freelancers and 750,000 active clients. Fiverr processed tens of millions of microtransactions across creative and technical tasks.

These platforms succeeded not just because they helped people find work, but because they made the act of delivering that work *usable*—for both the freelancer and the buyer.

And now, a similar transformation is beginning in AI.

While estimates vary, it's likely that 1.5 to 2 million freelance developers work in the U.S. alone, with many more worldwide. Thousands are now building AI-powered tools and agents using platforms like LangChain, Hugging Face, CrewAI, and open-source LLM frameworks. They're not building full-blown enterprise software—they're building something smaller, and in many ways more valuable: intelligent microservices, or what we've called throughout this book, AI Tasks.

These are focused tools that do things like:

- Summarize legal documents
- Score sales leads
- Automate email responses
- Generate job descriptions
- Parse PDFs for compliance language
- Match startups to funding criteria
- Provide rating and pricing information for insurance policies

But there's a problem. Building these tools is now easier than ever. Distributing and monetizing them is not.

Most development platforms—while powerful for experimentation—do little to support commerce or implementation. Tools like LangChain and AutoGPT help you build. But they don't help you sell. They don't help businesses discover your solution, activate it, pay for it, or trust that it will work in a real-world production environment.

There is no centralized marketplace.

No unified deployment mechanism.

No shared data permissioning system.

No billing, analytics, or usage tracking.

No one-click delivery.

And as a result, the tools themselves are scattered—living on GitHub, in Discord communities, or buried in niche app aggregators. Businesses that want to use them must often download code, manage environment variables, acquire API keys, or worse—hire someone to stitch it all together.

In short, AI is experiencing the same fragmentation that defined the early internet.

Back then, developers built widgets—contact forms, chat scripts, timers, signup pages—but there was no App Store. No plugin marketplace. No monetization system. Great tools existed. But they were inaccessible. It wasn't until platforms like WordPress, Shopify, and Apple's App Store emerged, over a decade or more after the internet in commerce got its foothold, that independent developers could scale their work—building once and selling to thousands.

We are at the same turning point in AI.

What's needed now is a unified platform where developers can:

- Build intelligent, secure, reusable AI Tasks
- Package them in a standardized framework
- List them in a trusted marketplace
- Monetize based on usage or business value
- Reach an audience of businesses who can activate with a click

And where businesses can:

- Browse solutions by need or industry
- See what a Task does, what it needs, and what it costs
- Use their own data, securely siloed and private
- Launch with no code, no consultants, and no delay
- Get outcomes—not just outputs

The freelance economy has already transformed how people work. Now, it's poised to transform how intelligence is delivered. Developers no longer need to build monolithic applications or join massive teams to create value. And businesses no longer need to wait months—or spend millions—to benefit from intelligent systems. What's missing isn't talent or tools. It's infrastructure. A bridge between those who build and those who need what's been built. As we saw with the rise of app stores and cloud marketplaces, the real breakthrough comes not from invention alone—but from distribution, discoverability, and trust. The next generation of AI platforms won't just empower freelancers to create—they'll empower them to participate in the economy of outcomes. And in doing so, they'll help reshape the very structure of work. This is not just a shift in technology. It's a shift in how value is created, shared, and scaled.

How Intelligent Business Management Platform™ Solutions Connect Developers with Businesses

In theory, the freelance AI economy should be thriving. Developers have the tools. Businesses have the needs. Yet the connection between the two often breaks down. Why? Because building an AI Task is only half the battle. To deliver real value, it also needs to be hosted securely, integrated seamlessly, and made easily accessible to end users.

This is where Intelligent Business Management Platform™ (IBMP) solutions change the equation.

These systems don't just facilitate AI Task development—they address the infrastructure problems that have long made custom automation difficult to scale. By solving for hosting, data access, and integration, IBMP solutions eliminate the friction between an idea and its implementation.

Let's break that down into the three foundational problems that IBMP solutions are designed to solve: hosting, data, and integration.

Smart Hosting: Bringing the Task Inside the Platform

When a freelance developer builds an AI Task, it needs a reliable home— somewhere it can run securely, perform consistently, and scale with demand. Traditional deployment approaches (cloud containers, external APIs, or self-hosted models) require businesses to manage configuration, security, and ongoing maintenance—barriers that quickly erode usability.

Smart Hosting, offered within Intelligent Business Management Platform™ solutions, solves this by allowing AI Tasks to be natively hosted inside the platform environment.

This creates a number of advantages:

- The Task is automatically compatible with other features and functions in the system.
- Developers can deploy without needing to manage infrastructure or external tooling.
- Businesses gain confidence that hosted Tasks are secure, stable, and governed by platform-wide standards.

In short, Smart Hosting allows AI Tasks to function as native components, not foreign add-ons. They operate like built-in features—without requiring the business to manage them.

Siloed Data Access: Secure, Contextual, and Controlled

The value of an AI Task depends not only on how it functions, but on the data it can access. Many promising tools fail because they lack access to the business's internal systems. Meanwhile, business leaders are rightfully cautious about allowing external code to process sensitive information.

Intelligent Business Management Platform™ solutions resolve this tension by providing secure, siloed data environments for each business, typically through internal vector databases or structured repositories. These environments allow Tasks to interact with data without compromising ownership, privacy, or compliance.

In practical terms:

- A document review Task can analyze actual business contracts without sending them outside the platform.

- A sales automation Task can reference the company's live CRM data—without needing external permissions.
- A reporting Task can pull from internal finance records without accessing other clients' information.

By embedding this access into the platform architecture, IBMP solutions create the conditions for secure, context-rich intelligence—without exposing businesses to risk.

AI-Supported Integration: Making Tasks Work Together, Automatically

Even the best AI Tasks are only effective if they can operate within the larger business workflow. Traditionally, integrating new tools—especially third-party ones—has been a slow, technical process involving APIs, custom scripting, or IT support.

Intelligent Business Management Platform™ solutions introduce AI-supported integration—a system-level feature that allows Tasks to configure themselves based on user settings, business context, and system logic.

That means:

- A new Task can detect where it fits in a workflow and connect itself accordingly.
- Data routing and output handling happen automatically—without manual setup.
- Tasks can interact with one another, triggering or feeding into each other as needed.

This enables not just automation, but orchestration, and is assembled in a very simple way. Multiple Tasks can collaborate to achieve business goals without the user needing to script or stitch them together.

One-Click Activation: From Developer to Business in Seconds

One-click activation, introduced in the last chapter, is the culmination of Smart Hosting, secure data access, and AI-supported integration.

When all the infrastructure is in place, activating a new Task becomes effortless. Businesses don't need IT teams, training manuals, or onboarding calls. They simply select a Task from the marketplace and click "activate."

From there:

- The Task is hosted natively within the Intelligent Business Management Platform™.
- It gains access to the appropriate siloed data.
- It begins operating within the existing workflow—immediately.

This transforms what was once a lengthy implementation process into a moment of action. Businesses no longer have to choose between speed and capability—they get both. And developers are no longer limited to sharing code—they can share real, ready-to-run solutions.

This is the potential of Intelligent Business Management Platform™ solutions: not only to support AI adoption, but to make it operational—by embedding the infrastructure, intelligence, and trust needed to turn AI into action.

The Power of a Task Marketplace

When businesses adopt new technology, the challenge is rarely a lack of tools. More often, it's the difficulty of identifying what's useful—and implementing it without friction. For developers, the challenge is almost the opposite: they're able to build powerful, high-value solutions, but frequently struggle to connect those solutions with the businesses that need them most.

A Task Marketplace solves both sets of problems.

By creating a curated space where intelligent AI Tasks can be curated, browsed, activated, and monetized, the marketplace becomes the connective tissue between freelance innovation and real business need. It offers visibility for developers and simplicity for business users—two things that rarely coexist in traditional software ecosystems.

At its core, the Task Marketplace model is a response to fragmentation. It eliminates the chaos of searching repositories, reviewing agency proposals, or building custom automation from scratch. Instead, it creates a centralized environment where:

- AI Tasks are packaged, described, and ready to activate.
- Businesses can explore solutions by function, outcome, or department.
- Tasks can be curated and recommended to a business based on their needs.
- Developers can build once and scale across thousands of users.
- Businesses can rely on one-click activation and native integration.
- Businesses can implement the AI Tasks or functions they need on a subscription or one-time basis, paying only for what they use.

This marketplace is more than a catalog—it is a discovery engine for intelligence.

Solving the Problem on Both Sides

For freelance developers, the marketplace answers the most pressing issue: distribution. Developers are often capable of building highly specialized and innovative tools—but lack access to customers, payment systems, or hosting infrastructure. The marketplace gives them a direct line to real business users. It allows them to price, publish, update, and track the usage of their work, with the same ease that an IOS app developer publishes to the Apple App Store.

For business users, the marketplace solves the equally important problem of access and integration. They no longer need to search for vendors, scope projects, or manage security and data flows. Instead, they enter a trusted platform environment, browse Tasks designed for their use case, and click to deploy. The Task is hosted, integrated, and powered by the same data infrastructure as the rest of the platform.

The Role of AI in the Marketplace

Of course, a marketplace can only scale if it avoids becoming overwhelming. Thousands—or eventually tens of thousands—of Tasks will live inside a mature platform. The key to maintaining clarity is not better filters; it's better intelligence.

To use our solution, LIBBi, as an example, our industry-first marketplace directly connects businesses with AI Task developers, the marketplace is enhanced by a built-in AI recommendation engine. This engine learns from the behavior of the business user, understands their structure, industry, and goals, and proactively suggests Tasks that align with their needs.

Rather than forcing the user to search for solutions, the platform surfaces them at the right moment. A business that recently onboarded a new employee might be shown Tasks related to access configuration, training workflows, or compliance documentation—before they even think to ask.

This recommendation engine keeps the business operating at the frontier of capability—always within reach of the state of the art.

Lessons from Other Industries

The Task Marketplace model is not unique to AI—it's the natural evolution of software ecosystems. And it's a model that has already transformed other industries.

- Retail: Amazon became dominant not by selling its own products, but by creating a marketplace where any vendor could participate. Its algorithms recommend what users need before they look for it.
- Transportation: Uber disrupted taxi services by turning transportation into a marketplace of freelance drivers, dynamically routed and surfaced through location-based AI.
- Tourism: Airbnb created a marketplace for space—offering tools for trust, listing, booking, and customer communication in one platform.
- Creative Services: Platforms like Fiverr and Upwork have created marketplaces where design, writing, and development talent can be discovered, reviewed, and engaged instantly.

What these platforms share is a structure that brings demand and supply together in a low-friction environment, supported by smart interfaces, secure systems, and intelligent recommendations.

The same logic applies to AI Tasks. The difference is that, instead of delivering goods or services, the Task Marketplace delivers intelligence—and does so at the speed and scale modern businesses now require.

In many ways, the Task Marketplace is the logical next step in the evolution of software delivery, especially in the age of AI for business. It abstracts away complexity, compresses time-to-value, and puts intelligence within immediate reach of the businesses that need it most. By uniting builders and users inside a shared ecosystem, it doesn't just solve for distribution or access—it reshapes how innovation moves. What once required weeks of scoping, contracting, and configuration can now happen in a click. And as AI Tasks become more powerful and more abundant, the marketplace ensures they remain usable, relevant, and context-aware.

From Ecosystem to Execution: Getting What Your Business Actually Needs

For decades, business leaders have faced a common frustration: they know what they want to improve, but they're limited by what their software can do. Whether it's automating a follow-up process, analyzing a niche data set, or creating a custom report, turning vision into action has typically required a drawn-out process—scoping requirements, hiring developers, coordinating integrations, and waiting months for results.

AI-native platforms are beginning to eliminate that gap.

Instead of relying solely on predefined tools, these platforms create a more fluid relationship between problem and solution. Users can describe what they need in natural language, and the platform can respond—either by routing the request to a developer within the ecosystem or, increasingly, by generating the solution itself using embedded AI.

Consider a regional logistics company that wants to improve how it handles late deliveries. Traditionally, this would require a lengthy process: gathering incident data, working with developers to build a custom tracking tool, integrating it into existing systems, and training staff on its use. But in an AI-native platform, the operations manager can simply describe the problem— "I want to automatically flag late deliveries, notify the customer, and generate a weekly summary report." Instantaneously, the platform recommends a pre-built AI Task that does exactly that. With one click, the task is activated, synced to the company's delivery data, and immediately begins identifying delays, sending branded email updates to customers, and compiling performance metrics. What once took months of planning now takes moments to implement—turning need into execution, not through a project, but through a platform.

This is not just a shift in functionality—it's a shift in how businesses relate to technology.

Building Solutions Within the Ecosystem

Many AI platforms now support a network of freelance developers who are already building inside the system. This means that when a business user requests a specific task—like flagging overdue invoices, summarizing client notes, or launching a compliance check—the request can be picked up and fulfilled within the platform environment itself.

The benefit isn't just speed (though the difference between 48 hours and six months is meaningful). It's clarity. Because these developers already

understand the platform's logic, structure, and data standards, the tools they build are natively compatible. There's no need for manual configuration or costly integration projects.

It's the difference between hiring a general contractor to build onto your home—and having a room added by the architect who designed the house in the first place.

Tasks Built by AI

Even more significant is what's happening at the edge of automation: platforms that can now generate business tools directly through AI.

As discussed in Chapter 4, generative AI has made it possible to describe a task and have the system construct it—automatically. And in Chapter 5, we explored how autonomous agents will evolve to anticipate and act without human prompting. Both of those developments are now converging in modern platforms.

A user might ask, "Can I tag invoices by category and get alerts when one exceeds $5,000?" In an AI-native platform, the system can now build that task—from the logic to the interface—without requiring a developer to touch it. The user doesn't need to know how it works. It just happens.

What used to take planning, coding, and deployment now takes a sentence.

This isn't simply convenient—it's a redefinition of business agility. It allows teams to go from friction to function in real time.

From Concept to Capability

This convergence of developer access and intelligent automation marks a turning point for organizations. It reframes how businesses evaluate technology—not just as something they adapt to, but something that adapts to them.

In platforms like the LIBBi Intelligent Business Management Platform™, business users don't just access tools. They participate in shaping them. Whether through a request routed to a developer within the LIBBi ecosystem, or through generative AI that builds the task directly, the result is the same: organizations get the specific intelligence they need, on demand.

This changes more than workflows—it changes mindset.

Instead of being constrained by what's already available, teams are encouraged to imagine what's possible. The software no longer defines the process; the business does. Requests that once required external vendors, internal approval cycles, or patchwork integrations are now answered in-platform, with tasks created, deployed, and maintained in a unified environment.

The result isn't just more automation. It's faster problem-solving. Leaner teams. Sharper execution.

And most importantly, it's the removal of the long-standing barrier between a business idea and its implementation.

Final Thoughts: Built for Business

The breakthroughs described in this chapter don't just signal a shift in software—they signal a shift in power.

For decades, intelligence in business was something you had to license, customize, or wait for. It came wrapped in bloated systems, slow timelines, and the need for intermediaries. But in this new model—powered by AI Tasks, distributed development, and Intelligent Business Management Platforms™—intelligence becomes something far more immediate. Far more personal. It becomes something you can *use* without asking for permission.

And on the other side of that interface, something equally profound is happening: the rise of the freelance AI developer.

These builders—independent, entrepreneurial, and often working alone—have been living on the creative edge of what's possible. They are the modern craftspeople of intelligence, using LLMs, APIs, and open frameworks to design solutions no traditional software vendor would ever build. Not because those ideas weren't valuable—but because they weren't scalable by legacy standards. Now, all of that changes.

With the emergence of AI-native platforms and task-based marketplaces, freelance developers can build once and distribute infinitely. They can monetize without fundraising, scale without infrastructure, and deliver impact without needing a sales team. In many ways, this is the culmination of a movement: the legitimization of the independent technologist—not just as a gig worker, but as a force of innovation. Not just as a coder, but as a product creator. These aren't side hustlers. They are software entrepreneurs. And for the first time, there's a system built to empower their economy.

On the other side, business leaders finally get the one thing they've always needed: traction. Not demos. Not delays. But real, measurable outcomes—

delivered through intelligent tasks that work from day one and evolve as the business evolves.

The result is a new ecosystem of mutual empowerment. Developers are free to build. Businesses are free to act. And platforms become the connective tissue that holds it all together—with hosting, data access, integration, and trust built in from the start.

This is how intelligence now moves—freely, frictionlessly, and at scale.

The future of business software won't be dominated by a few monoliths—it will be defined by thousands of intelligent microservices, built by a global network of problem-solvers and orchestrated by the businesses that use them. It won't be about which company has the most tools. It will be about which leader knows how to use them best.

Because when execution is just one click away, imagination becomes strategy—and innovation becomes inevitable.

Chapter 8: Securing the Future — Data Control, Compliance, and Trust

In 2018, the world witnessed a reckoning.

The Cambridge Analytica scandal didn't just dominate headlines—it triggered global outrage, wiped billions from Facebook's valuation, and forced a new conversation about data ethics into the public square. What began as a breach of user privacy quickly evolved into a deeper, more urgent question: *Who controls our data—and what responsibility comes with that control?*

That question has only grown more relevant in the age of artificial intelligence.

When we talk about "data" in a business context, we're talking about the digital footprint your company leaves as it operates: customer contact records, sales transactions, invoices, website traffic, employee activity, internal emails. It's the sum total of what your business knows, captures, and creates. Every price you set, every form you submit, every customer interaction—it all generates data. And in the AI era, that data becomes more than just information. It becomes intelligence. It fuels predictions, powers automation, and enables businesses to move with greater speed, precision, and personalization than ever before.

But with that power comes a new kind of responsibility.

Over the last several chapters, we've explored how AI Tasks are created, activated, and orchestrated. We've seen how intelligent platforms like LIBBi are helping businesses move from manual processes to dynamic systems. But none of that transformation means anything—none of it endures—without trust.

And in the era of AI, trust begins and ends with data.

This chapter is about that foundation. It's about what it means to build systems that are not only powerful, but principled. It's about control, compliance, and accountability—and how each of these contributes to business resilience. We'll explore how intelligent platforms consolidate data responsibly, how ethical frameworks are becoming competitive differentiators, and how a new kind of "trust premium" is beginning to define the most successful companies in the AI economy.

You'll learn:

- Why centralized, structured data environments are essential for AI to deliver consistent value

- How secure architectures—like the one powering LIBBi—can offer real-time intelligence without sacrificing privacy

- What every business leader needs to understand about evolving regulations, responsible AI use, and the hidden risks inside many LLM and SaaS tools

- And why trust isn't just a legal box to check—but a strategic asset to protect and scale

In the next era of business, success won't belong only to those with the best tools or the fastest automation. It will belong to the businesses their customers *trust*—to use data wisely, securely, and ethically.

Because in a world increasingly run by algorithms, character still matters.

The Data Foundation: Why Consolidation Matters

At the heart of every AI-powered business system lies the same critical asset: data. But not just any data—consolidated, structured, and accessible data. Without it, AI isn't intelligent—it's blind.

In traditional business environments, data fragmentation has been the norm. Customer messages live in the customer relationship management system (CRM) like HubSpot or Sales Force. Inventory is tracked in a separate ERP. Invoicing happens through accounting software like Quick Books. Reservations and schedules through a yet another system like Toast. Employee data sits in HRIS platforms. Marketing runs off campaign tools, while analytics are handled somewhere else entirely.

Each system may perform well in isolation. But for a business trying to operate in real-time, respond intelligently, or automate decision-making, this patchwork creates friction at every turn.

And now, we're seeing this problem repeat itself in the world of AI.

Many of today's AI tools create new data—but they don't consolidate it, a refrain you have now heard mentioned several times in this book. Each chatbot, analytics dashboard, or automation tool stores outputs in its own silo. These outputs can't be easily shared across systems. There is no shared context. Fragmentation isn't just a byproduct—it's baked into the model. And it severely limits what AI can do.

We've seen this before.

In the late 1990s and early 2000s, Borders Group—one of the largest book retailers in the world—failed to consolidate its digital operations. It outsourced its online presence to Amazon, treating e-commerce as an isolated function instead of a strategic core. Its inventory systems weren't fully integrated with its customer database, and pricing decisions happened without coordination between digital and physical channels. The result? Borders couldn't see its own business clearly, and it was overtaken by more data-integrated competitors. It filed for bankruptcy in 2011.

Contrast that with Walmart, a company that invested heavily in centralized data infrastructure long before it was trendy. Walmart built one of the world's most advanced supply chain and inventory systems, enabling real-time insights across thousands of locations. Their data architecture connected procurement, logistics, sales, pricing, and even employee scheduling. This consolidation allowed them to operate with precision, cut costs, and respond to consumer demand faster than competitors. It wasn't just about scale—it was about integration. And it worked.

The lesson is simple but profound: data consolidation isn't a technical preference—it's another strategic advantage.

AI Tasks, in particular, rely on context. A Task designed to forecast revenue can only be effective if it can access current contracts, recent invoice trends, and customer churn rates. A compliance Task needs visibility into document histories, regulatory updates, and employee acknowledgments. Without access to the right data, in the right format, at the right time, even the smartest AI underperforms.

This is where the right AI solution can represent a generational shift in architecture.

Rather than layering AI tools on top of fragmented systems, unified and thoughtful AI solutions create a central data architecture by design. As an example, but certainly not the only AI system to consolidate data, the Intelligent Business Management Platform™ solutions contain exactly the architecture to achieve consolidation by design. From the moment a business begins using the platform, a secure, siloed database is created—dedicated entirely to that business. This becomes the data foundation for everything that follows.

Each time the business activates a new AI Task—whether for onboarding, sales outreach, pricing analysis, or invoice reconciliation—that Task is not only consuming data from the repository, it's also adding to it. Outputs, interactions, decisions, logs, and metadata are all written back into the centralized store.

The result is a living repository of institutional knowledge. It's searchable, trainable, and accessible—governed by permissions, secured by role-based access controls (RBAC), and completely isolated from other businesses.

Because every Task draws from and contributes to the same source, integration becomes automatic.

Imagine, for example, a Product Pricing Task. In a typical SaaS environment, that Task would need to integrate with your invoicing platform to understand past sales, query your CRM to evaluate upcoming demand, and reference spreadsheets or external dashboards for cost data. But in an IBMP, it doesn't need to integrate—it simply has access.

- It sees completed sales via the Invoicing Task.
- It tracks cost margins from the Finance Task.
- It forecasts product demand through insights generated by the Sales Pipeline Task.

- It even accounts for seasonal trends or promotional impact through data generated by the Marketing Campaign Task.

And it does all of this without stitching systems together or passing through external APIs. The data is already consolidated. The logic is already compatible. The context is already available.

This is the promise of AI that works like a team member—not because it's human-like, but because it understands the entire business. Not just a slice of it.

This kind of consolidation has another major benefit: governance.

Because data lives in a single, structured repository, platforms can enforce security and compliance consistently. Smart Hosting ensures that Tasks operate inside controlled environments. Access tokens (like JWT) define who can view or modify data. Role Based Access Control policies ensure that only the right people—and the right AI Tasks—can touch the information they need. Nothing leaks. Nothing floats in the cloud unaccounted for.

The conclusion is clear: if your AI tools are running on fragmented data, they will produce fragmented outcomes.

But if they run on a shared foundation—built for visibility, speed, and security—they become more than tools. They become strategic infrastructure.

The Trust Premium: Why Security Is Now a Differentiator

In her book *Trustworthy AI*, Beena Ammanath argues that trust is not a side effect of well-built technology—it's the central requirement. In the age of artificial intelligence, trust has become a strategic asset, a product feature, and a market differentiator all at once. But it's not just about technical precision. It's about relational trust: Do users understand how the system works? Do they feel safe? Do they believe that their data, their autonomy, and their expectations are respected?

This is where many AI platforms still fall short.

Too often, AI is deployed as a black box. It takes in data, processes it invisibly, and produces results without explanation. There's no audit trail. No way to interrogate how a decision was made. No clear boundaries on where data lives, who can access it, or how long it's stored.

That opacity breeds hesitation—and hesitation kills adoption.

On the other hand, platforms that build transparency, auditability, and user control into their core design earn what we call, and borrow the term, the "trust premium." These platforms aren't just compliant—they are trusted. Their customers are more engaged, their enterprise clients are more loyal, and their reputations are more resilient.

It is our view that business solutions should be designed to achieve the trust premium intentionally. To do so, every layer should be thoughtfully considered and work together to achieve the desired result. Things like Smart Hosting, which isolates data environments per business, to Role-Based Access Control (RBAC) that limits user permissions, SOC 2 certification, all make a difference. Let's dig a little deeper into some of these trust-enhancing considerations.

Understanding SOC 2 and the Rise of Compliance as a Business Strategy

For years, compliance was seen as a back-office requirement—something you addressed after product launch, or during due diligence. Today, that has changed. In the age of AI, compliance is becoming a business strategy in itself. It's a signal of maturity, readiness, and trustworthiness in a world where data is both a business asset and a point of vulnerability.

One of the most prominent standards driving this shift is SOC 2, a globally recognized sign of excellence in terms of security.

Developed by the American Institute of CPAs (AICPA), SOC 2 stands for "Service Organization Control 2"—but what it really stands for is trust. SOC 2 isn't a software test or a technical checklist. It's a holistic audit of how a company manages customer data, across people, processes, and platforms.

What makes SOC 2 so powerful is that it's built around five fundamental "Trust Services Criteria", which serve as the backbone of modern data stewardship:

1.	Security – Is the system protected against unauthorized access, both physical and digital? This principle examines firewalls, authentication, intrusion detection, and more.

2.	Availability – Is the system available for operation and use as committed or agreed? This covers uptime commitments, disaster recovery, and performance monitoring.

3.	Processing Integrity – Are system operations accurate, complete, and timely? This ensures that data is processed exactly as it should be—without loss, duplication, or corruption.

4.   Confidentiality – Is confidential business and personal data appropriately safeguarded? This includes encryption, access control, and contractual protections.

5.   Privacy – Is personal information collected, used, and retained according to principles that respect user consent and legal compliance?

Together, these principles form the foundation of trustworthy digital infrastructure. A successful SOC 2 audit sends a clear message to customers, partners, and investors alike: *this business is serious about protecting data.*

It's no surprise, then, that adoption of SOC 2 is growing rapidly—especially among SaaS and cloud-native businesses. According to recent industry estimates, nearly 70% of large companies either hold or are actively pursuing SOC 2 certification. For enterprises that serve regulated industries—finance, healthcare, legal—the number is even higher.

But the story is more complex for small and medium size businesses.

For these teams, the demands of SOC 2 can feel overwhelming. Achieving certification requires documenting processes, monitoring access, deploying secure architecture, and—perhaps most challenging—proving that your team follows these practices consistently over time. SOC 2 is not a "one and done" check. It's a continuous commitment.

For many businesses, this is simply out of reach. The cost of a SOC 2 audit can exceed $50,000, and the preparation can take 6–12 months—even longer without dedicated compliance staff. As a result, SOC 2 has traditionally been seen as a milestone for companies that have already reached a certain size.

But that, too, is changing.

As customers become more discerning, and as regulators tighten expectations, trust is becoming a differentiator—especially for AI platforms. For what it's worth, if it was not obvious, we are strong advocates for every solution category servicing business to adopt this standard or further innovate to continue raising the bar. By embedding SOC 2-aligned infrastructure from day one—through features like Smart Hosting, Role-Based Access Control (RBAC), and real-time audit logging—platforms can extend security and compliance to their users, even if those users are small businesses without in-house expertise.

And the shift toward "trust-as-a-service" has a powerful precedent.

Former U.S. Under Secretary of State and DocuSign chairman Keith Krach, in numerous public addresses, has emphasized that *"trust is the most powerful currency in the world."* In his work on trusted technology standards and digital trust diplomacy, Krach outlined what he called the Trust Principle—a framework that elevates transparency, accountability, respect for human rights, and rule-of-law alignment as essential traits for technology governance. His message is simple: trust must be earned, and systems that cannot prove they are trustworthy will not survive the next wave of scrutiny. Krach's Trust Principles are broader than data integrity, although an essential part, but his work makes exactly the right point about the importance of trust in today's digital world.

That's why SOC 2—and standards like it—aren't just for compliance officers. They're for everyone who wants to build something that lasts.

In effect, a well-designed and unified business solution can provide enterprise-grade trust architecture to businesses of all sizes. A solo entrepreneur on Day 1 has access to the same compliance-grade infrastructure as a 500-person company. This not only simplifies deployment—it accelerates growth. Because the faster a business can prove it is trustworthy, the faster it can scale partnerships, win contracts, and serve regulated clients.

Understanding GDPR: A Global Signal of Respect and Responsibility

While SOC 2 is a widely recognized standard for data security and operational integrity, another critical framework—especially for businesses with customers in Europe—is GDPR, or the General Data Protection Regulation. We provided a general overview of GDPR in Chapter 2, but its relevance and importance should be clearer to you given the information you've consumed over the past few chapters. Passed by the European Union in 2016 and enforced since 2018, GDPR is a law that gives individuals greater control over their personal data and holds businesses to higher standards of transparency, consent, and accountability.

Put simply, GDPR is about respecting people's data as if it were your own. It requires businesses to clearly explain what data they collect, why they collect it, how long they keep it, and who they share it with. It also gives customers the right to see, correct, delete, or limit the use of their information at any time. For businesses, this means no more vague fine print or assumptions of consent—data relationships must be clear, honest, and optional.

From a practical standpoint, GDPR compliance may involve changes to how your business gathers customer information (such as adding opt-in checkboxes), stores records (ensuring secure systems and regular audits), and responds to requests (such as deleting data upon customer demand). While the law is European, its impact is global—because any company that markets to or serves EU residents must comply, regardless of where the business is based.

Just like SOC 2, GDPR isn't just about avoiding penalties—it's about earning trust in a digital-first world. A GDPR-compliant business signals to its customers that it takes their privacy seriously and is willing to go the extra mile to protect it. And in a time when data misuse can destroy reputations overnight, showing that your business follows global best practices for privacy is no longer optional—it's a competitive advantage.

The Strategic Value of Data Security and Privacy:

In *AI Data Privacy and Protection*, authors Justin Ryan and Mario Lazo make a provocative but increasingly validated claim: privacy is not merely a compliance issue—it's a strategic asset. Businesses that treat data ethics as a design principle, not just a legal obligation, consistently outperform their peers. The advantage is not philosophical. It's operational. It's reputational. And increasingly, it's financial.

Why? Because companies that prioritize ethical data practices enjoy a compound benefit:

- They attract higher-quality customers—buyers who are more engaged, more loyal, and more discerning. In a landscape flooded with AI-powered tools, trust becomes the ultimate differentiator.
- They retain those users longer—because trust, once earned, increases user satisfaction, reduces churn, and creates what Ryan and Lazo refer to as "compliance stickiness."
- They reduce their exposure to risk—not just in fines or legal action, but in reputational fallout. A data breach today is not a technical error—it's a brand failure.

- They empower their teams to innovate safely—because clear ethical frameworks allow fast decisions without crossing lines. Guardrails don't slow progress—they accelerate it.

In that sense, ethical data practices are not just about avoiding what could go wrong. They're about enabling what can go right. They create the conditions for speed, innovation, and scale—because they replace fear with clarity, ambiguity with confidence.

This aligns directly with what Intelligent Business Management Platform™ solutions and other business solutions that adopt similar standards are designed to do. By embedding transparency, traceability, and data siloing into the architecture itself, IBMPs make it easier for businesses to build fast without cutting corners. Every AI Task is governed by a common framework. Every interaction is auditable. Every data access point is secured. This architecture doesn't just comply with privacy best practices—it codifies them.

Contrast this with traditional systems, where ethical data use depends on training, policy enforcement, and patchwork integration across tools that don't talk to one another. In that environment, mistakes are inevitable—and trust is fragile. But when data ethics is built into the platform, not added after the fact, responsibility becomes scalable.

The companies that win in AI will not be those that run the fastest. They will be those that run the cleanest, with the greatest clarity and the least friction. Because in a world where algorithms can be copied and intelligence commodified, the true competitive edge comes from how responsibly that intelligence is managed.

Data ethics is no longer a sideline conversation. It is now a core strategy. And it's one of the clearest markers of which businesses are truly built for the future.

The Invisible Risk: Data Exposure in LLM-Based Tools

As generative AI and large language models (LLMs) become more integrated into business tools, a new form of risk has emerged—data invisibility. Businesses are increasingly wary of uploading sensitive or proprietary information into LLM-based systems, not because the technology lacks capability, but because it lacks transparency. When a company inputs financial records, internal strategy documents, or client communications into an LLM interface, it's rarely clear what happens next. Is the data stored? Is it used to train future models? Who has access to it on the backend? These are critical questions—often left unanswered.

The problem intensifies with LLM-wrapped platforms and AI-powered SaaS tools that layer branded interfaces on top of generalized models. While these products may promise productivity gains, many do so without publishing clear security protocols, data handling practices, or compliance certifications. Businesses are asked to trust invisible infrastructure. And in doing so, they risk violating client confidentiality, breaching contractual obligations, or exposing trade secrets—all without any formal breach necessarily occurring.

This lack of clarity poses a particularly acute risk for organizations in regulated industries like healthcare, finance, legal, and government contracting. Even if the LLM tool performs well, the inability to trace where the data goes, how long it's retained, and what governance applies creates both operational and ethical uncertainty. In the absence of published security

standards or third-party audits (such as SOC 2 or ISO 27001), businesses are left to hope—rather than verify—that their data remains protected.

This is why many forward-looking businesses are rejecting black-box models in favor of platforms that are designed with transparency, control, and compliance at the core. The ability to see, manage, and contain data flows is no longer a "nice-to-have"—it's essential.

When Trust Breaks: The Story of Finwell Capital

In 2021, Finwell Capital, a fast-scaling financial services company specializing in small business lending, became a cautionary tale in the world of data security. After tripling its customer base during the pandemic through aggressive digital onboarding and automation, Finwell turned to several AI-powered SaaS platforms to streamline operations—ranging from lead qualification to risk modeling. These third-party tools were selected for speed and ease-of-use, but many lacked clear privacy protocols, data ownership transparency, or even defined hosting parameters.

What Finwell failed to recognize was that in uploading sensitive financial data—including business tax records, credit histories, and scanned identification—to these platforms, they were effectively handing over control to black-box systems. One such vendor experienced a breach through a misconfigured server. The breach exposed more than 1.2 million loan applicant records—including Social Security numbers, bank statements, and internal approval workflows. It took Finwell weeks to uncover the scope of the leak, and even longer to trace its source due to the absence of centralized logging or role-based access control.

The costs were severe. Finwell faced multiple class-action lawsuits, regulatory penalties from the FTC and state financial regulators, and an exodus of clients—particularly among minority-owned businesses who felt betrayed by the mishandling of their most personal information. The company's valuation dropped by 42% in six months, and its attempts to raise a new funding round failed. Customers cited a loss of trust, not just in Finwell's tools, but in its culture and leadership.

Though Finwell did eventually recover—after restructuring leadership and investing millions into a new security framework—it had to rebuild from the ground up. Ironically, the post-crisis audits concluded that had the company adopted a platform architected with security in mind from day one, such as siloed data containers, built-in audit trails, and the right architecture, the breach would have been avoidable. The patchwork use of third-party SaaS tools had created a web of dependencies, each with unclear data handling protocols and no enforceable privacy safeguards.

This stands in stark contrast to what businesses experience when using many generic LLM-based AI services or SaaS platforms today. These tools may be branded as "AI-enabled," but they often require businesses to upload customer data into opaque systems that use pooled models or shared training environments. Data might be stored indefinitely, used to improve the vendor's algorithms, or transferred across jurisdictions—all without explicit permission or user awareness. In such environments, data ownership becomes ambiguous, and businesses may unknowingly expose themselves to reputational or legal risk.

Platforms designed around transparent, localized, and controllable data governance models eliminate that ambiguity. Instead of trusting that a vendor will "do the right thing," businesses using such platforms see what happens to their data, who accesses it, and why. This difference isn't just technical—it's cultural. And in an era where trust is a market advantage, it may be the single most important architectural decision a business can make.

Case Study: Secure by Design

As artificial intelligence capabilities expand, so too do the stakes for data protection, control, and ethical use. The question facing businesses is no longer limited to what a platform can *do*—but rather, *how* it does it, *where* the data resides, *who* can access it, and *what mechanisms* are in place to preserve integrity and privacy. In this context, data architecture is not simply a technical construct—it is a governance framework and a risk mitigation imperative.

The Intelligent Business Management Platform™ (IBMP) solution, LIBBi, offers a unique case study in secure-by-design infrastructure. Rather than bolting security features onto an existing system, LIBBi embeds privacy, trust, and data protection directly into its architectural DNA. This design choice reflects a shift in paradigm: from reactive compliance to proactive trust architecture.

At the foundation of LIBBi's data strategy is the principle of data sovereignty—the idea that businesses should maintain full ownership and transparent control over the data they generate. To actualize this, LIBBi employs a siloed container model, in which each business operates within its own isolated vector database. This guarantees that no records are shared, co-mingled, or used to train cross-tenant models. It also eliminates the possibility of accidental data exposure between accounts—an ongoing vulnerability in many SaaS systems.

Beyond isolation, LIBBi implements end-to-end encryption protocols and enforces strict authentication measures. The platform uses secure digital ID badges to make sure only the right people—or approved AI Tasks—can access specific information. It also follows strict rules based on job roles, so employees and systems can only see the data they need to do their work. This helps keep sensitive business and customer information safe and under control.

LIBBi takes things a step further with what it calls Smart Hosting. This means every AI tool runs safely inside LIBBi's own protected environment, instead of relying on outside systems that could pose security risks. Unlike other platforms that send your data out to third-party services, LIBBi keeps your data in one secure place—and only shares it when you give clear permission. This design greatly reduces the chances of data leaks or outside interference.

Importantly, LIBBi's data architecture aligns with modern privacy and compliance standards. Its framework supports SOC 2 and GDPR-aligned practices, such as data minimization, incident transparency, and auditability. The system not only tracks access and changes through audit logs, but also enforces multi-factor authentication (MFA) and consent-based data policies. These features exemplify what governance scholar Keith Krach has called the "Trust Principle"—a model of technology design centered on transparency, accountability, and the ethical stewardship of information.

The broader implication is this: LIBBi demonstrates that data trustworthiness can be architected, not just promised. By treating security and privacy as foundational elements rather than afterthoughts, the platform serves as a model for how Intelligent Business Management Platforms™ can deliver both operational intelligence and institutional assurance.

Final Thoughts: Security and Privacy Are Now Strategic Imperatives

In today's data-driven economy, every business bears the responsibility of safeguarding its customers' information. This responsibility is no longer confined to IT departments or compliance teams—it has become a core leadership issue, a strategic risk vector, and a defining factor in long-term success. The decisions a business makes around data privacy and security reflect its values, its priorities, and its readiness to operate in a world where digital trust is paramount.

The rapid adoption of artificial intelligence and automation tools has only heightened this responsibility. Modern AI systems depend on access to vast amounts of sensitive and proprietary data to deliver value. But without visibility into how that data is managed, where it goes, and who can access it, businesses risk ceding control to opaque systems that may unintentionally violate customer trust, legal requirements, or industry standards.

Security and privacy can no longer be treated as afterthoughts. They must be designed into the very architecture of a business's technology stack. Organizations that wait to address these issues reactively—after a breach, a compliance failure, or a customer backlash—pay a steep price not only in financial penalties but in brand damage, lost trust, and reduced competitive positioning.

Conversely, businesses that proactively adopt technologies built with strong governance, transparent data handling, and embedded compliance frameworks signal maturity and foresight. They protect not only their systems but their relationships. They empower innovation by removing ambiguity and building confidence into every interaction with data.

In the era of AI for business, data governance is not just a technical concern—it is a strategic differentiator. The question is no longer whether businesses need to protect their data, but how intentionally and effectively they will do so. In the end, those who build trust into the foundation of their operations will be the ones best positioned to thrive in a future where trust is currency.

As this chapter concludes, so too does Section III: Understanding the AI Landscape. We've explored the foundations of intelligent platforms, the architecture of trust, and the critical importance of secure, ethical data use in business. These are not abstract principles—they are the groundwork for real-world transformation.

With this understanding in place, we now turn the page to Section IV: The Future of Work and the Intelligent Workforce. In Chapter 9, we will examine how AI is not just changing the tools we use—but redefining the very nature of work itself. As task automation accelerates, the human role is shifting—from execution to oversight, from routine to strategy. The next frontier is not just about adopting AI—it's about learning how to collaborate with it.

Part IV: The Future of Work and the Intelligent Workforce

Chapter 9: Redefining Work

In 1943, a young British mathematician named Mary Cartwright was recruited to support a secret wartime effort. Her role wasn't to build machines or break codes directly. Instead, she was tasked with something subtler—and ultimately more transformative: interpreting the emerging patterns produced by the primitive precursors to modern computers. Working alongside Alan Turing's team, Cartwright helped spot anomalies, refine tactics, and guide strategic decisions. She wasn't doing the work *for* the machines. She was doing the work *with* them. And that distinction made all the difference.

Nearly a century later, we find ourselves at a similar inflection point—but now, it's playing out on a global scale.

Welcome to Part IV: The Future of Work and the Intelligent Workforce.

In the chapters ahead, we explore how artificial intelligence is reshaping more than just workflows or software tools. It's reshaping the very definition of work itself—what it means to contribute, to lead, and to build enduring organizations in a world where machines can think, adapt, and act alongside us.

The role of the human professional is not vanishing—it's evolving. From execution to oversight. From repetition to strategy. From checking boxes to creating outcomes.

This transformation is already underway. AI is writing emails, routing support tickets, optimizing prices, and managing inventory. But the businesses leading this shift understand something essential: while machines can handle tasks, only people can provide vision. Judgment. Empathy. Culture. The things that make a business not just efficient, but exceptional.

Chapter 9 opens this section by asking a foundational question: What is work in the AI era?

We'll explore how the value of human effort is shifting, how intelligent systems are repositioning human contribution, and how leaders can build teams that thrive in a hybrid, human+AI environment. Grounded in new research and real-world applications, this chapter lays the foundation for a more intelligent, more resilient, and more human future of work.

Because in this next era, we're not replacing people.

We're reimagining what they're capable of.

The Current State of the Workforce and Technology

Across industries and professions, a simple truth is becoming increasingly clear: those who understand systems—how they connect, how they automate, and how they produce outcomes—already have a distinct advantage in today's workforce and will lead in this age. This holds true whether you're working at a corporate desk, on a construction site, in a classroom, or in the cockpit of an aircraft. In fields like law, healthcare, finance, construction, or education, technology is no longer just a department—it has become the infrastructure of daily operations, decision-making, and competitive advantage, and the era of AI for business has only just begun.

The current systems infrastructure asks all of us to navigate a growing web of platforms—CRM systems, AI agents, cloud software, collaborative dashboards—and to understand not only how to use them, but how they integrate across workflows. Familiarity with automation tools, data analytics, and intelligent systems is now as essential as traditional subject-matter expertise. And yet, many workers and leaders alike remain uncomfortable with this transition—one that began decades ago and is accelerating with the rise of AI. That discomfort is not a matter of capability or intelligence. It's a reflection of how quickly the systems have evolved, often without adequate training or without living up to the promises of simplicity and efficiency.

I've seen this shift up close. When I was in law school at Loyola University Chicago in the early 2000s, I was part of one of the last generations of students trained to use both the traditional legal library—a full floor of case reporters, statutes, and secondary sources—and the emerging digital research systems like LexisNexis and Westlaw. We learned to walk the stacks, follow citations through printed volumes, and feel the weight of the law—literally—in our hands. Everyone knew that the traditional methods were already fading, yet our professors and many practicing attorneys still clung tightly to them. As students, we were expected to learn both. That meant mastering Boolean logic, advanced filters, and digital search functions, while still appreciating the craftsmanship of book-based legal research.

That dual fluency—*book-based and tech-enabled*—became foundational to how we practiced law. We could still do the research the old way, but we could now do it faster, more strategically, and with greater reach thanks to digital systems that put precedent and analysis at our fingertips. I'll admit—somewhat sheepishly—that I even enjoyed the old way. There was something grounding about the quiet pursuit through shelves of knowledge.

But the truth is, I rarely used that skill again in my years of in-house practice. The world had moved on—and so had the work.

That experience taught me two things that remain as true today as ever: systems knowledge is a force multiplier, and the need to adapt is inevitable. The same legal insight delivered faster through better tools meant more time for strategy, better service to clients, and stronger preparation. And today, that same principle applies across every business function. The tools may be different in more expansive—what was Westlaw and LexisNexis in the early legal days is now Slack, HubSpot, Notion, Salesforce for many industries or LIBBi for business—but the core lesson holds: the more you understand the tools, the more valuable your thinking becomes and the more you can get done. And no matter how much I may have liked the books, progress was coming—with or without my permission.

In today's workforce the most empowered workers are those who combine professional judgment with technological fluency. AI will not change this valuation, it will only accentuate it further. These individuals won't be replaced by AI—they'll be elevated by it. As AI takes over more of the execution, human roles will become more strategic, more evaluative, and more essential.

Which Professions Will Be Most Impacted by AI?

As artificial intelligence becomes more capable and accessible, its impact is spreading across nearly every profession—but not all roles are affected equally. The degree to which a job is disrupted depends on several factors: how routine the work is, how dependent it is on structured data, and how easily parts of it can be automated or enhanced by intelligent systems.

According to a 2023 report from Goldman Sachs, as many as 300 million jobs globally could be exposed to some form of automation due to generative AI. However, the report emphasizes that exposure does not necessarily mean elimination. In most cases, AI will alter workflows—not replace them entirely. The World Economic Forum in 2023 similarly notes that while 44% of worker skills will be disrupted within five years, AI is expected to create new roles even as it transforms existing ones. According to the World Economic Forum's *Future of Jobs Report 2025*, approximately 40% of employers expect to reduce their workforce where AI can automate tasks.

So, which professions are feeling the effects most acutely?

Knowledge Workers in High-Exposure Roles

Professions such as legal services, financial analysis, marketing, and customer service are among the most exposed to AI automation. These fields rely heavily on information processing, written communication, pattern recognition, and rule-based logic—all areas where generative AI excels. A study by Eloundou et al. in 2023 found that legal, accounting, and administrative support roles are especially susceptible to large language models (LLMs), with over 80% of task functions potentially influenced by generative AI technologies.

Sales and Customer Experience

Routine customer service tasks are already being automated via chatbots, virtual assistants, and voice agents. But AI isn't just handling FAQs—it's now assisting with sentiment analysis, dynamic pricing, lead qualification, and even real-time sales coaching. According to a 2024 McKinsey report, AI-powered customer service transformations have led to a 40–50% reduction in service interactions and more than a 20% reduction in cost-to-serve, highlighting the significant impact of AI on customer engagement strategies. These advancements free human agents to focus on high-empathy, high-impact work, enhancing overall customer satisfaction.

Creative and Media Professions

Not surprisingly, the creative sector—writers, designers, editors, and content producers—is also deeply impacted. AI can now generate copy, design visuals, and even produce music and video. While this may seem threatening, experts like Paul Daugherty and H. James Wilson, in *Humans + Machines*, argue that creative professions will evolve, not vanish. Those who learn to co-create with AI will find their work scaled and enhanced, not replaced. Recent studies support this almost seven year-old perspective; for instance, a 2025 study published in *ScienceDirect* highlights that while generative AI adoption poses challenges, it also offers opportunities for creative professionals to enhance their work through collaboration with AI tools.

Healthcare and Diagnostics

In healthcare, AI is not replacing doctors, but it is reshaping how care is delivered. Tools like diagnostic imaging models, patient triage systems, and robotic surgery assistants are becoming standard. According to a 2024 systematic review published in *npj Digital Medicine*, AI diagnostic tools have demonstrated performance comparable to that of physicians in various medical specialties, including dermatology and radiology. The study found that while AI models matched the diagnostic accuracy of non-expert physicians, they still lagged behind expert clinicians, underscoring the importance of human oversight in clinical decision-making. These findings

highlight AI's potential to augment healthcare delivery, particularly in settings with limited access to specialist expertise.

Skilled Trades and Manual Labor

On the other end of the spectrum, skilled trades and manual labor roles are among the least impacted—at least for now. Jobs in construction, plumbing, electrical work, and caregiving rely on physical dexterity, spatial reasoning, and real-world problem solving—all areas where AI still struggles. However, as robotics advances, even these sectors will likely experience gradual change through AI-assisted diagnostics, materials optimization, and safety monitoring.

A Reframing, Not a Replacement

It's important to remember that AI does not simply eliminate jobs—it reshapes them. As Daniel Susskind puts it in *A World Without Work*, "The threat that technology poses to work is not that there will be no jobs, but that the nature of work will change, often in ways we are not prepared for."

This shift requires more than just new tools—it requires a new mindset. Professionals across every industry must invest in digital fluency, adaptability, and strategic thinking. The individuals who will thrive in this new landscape are not those who resist AI, but those who learn how to guide it, audit its output, and embed it intelligently into their workflows. They won't just keep up—they'll lead the transformation.

And that brings us back to a core idea introduced in Chapter 1: leadership is not an inherent trait—it's a learned skill. It's developed through intentional practice, continuous growth, and a clear understanding of one's environment. In that sense, the ability to lead—especially in the age of AI—becomes one of the most valuable, irreplaceable human capabilities we have.

Understanding the tools of today is no longer optional. It's the foundation for understanding the jobs of tomorrow. As AI systems become more capable and more deeply embedded in daily operations, the very structure of work is beginning to shift. But this shift isn't uniform. It's arriving unevenly across sectors, impacting some professions more directly—and more immediately—than others.

To prepare for what comes next, we need to start with clarity. That means taking an honest look at where AI is already reshaping the workforce—and where the next wave of transformation is poised to land.

Case Study: Human and Machine, a Powerful Combination

We would like to dig a bit deeper into the solution we have offered to the market to illustrate how the Intelligent Business Management Platform™ can both support and enhance this transition – for the benefit of us humans. The LIBBi platform was built from the ground up with this shift in mind. Its goal is not to replace human intelligence, but to amplify it—by automating execution, orchestrating intelligent workflows via thoughtful AI Tasks, and allowing humans to focus on high-value decisions.

At the solution's most basic level, the availability of AI supported Tasks useful in almost every workforce discipline provide huge efficiency and performance gains for workers who put them into action. The financial analysis that previously took an accounting professional an afternoon to assemble can be done in seconds using the right Task, coordinating the schedule of a service professional that previously took the office manager two hours is done automatically using the right LIBBi Task.

These efficiency gains are further advanced by Task Orchestration. In LIBBi, Tasks don't operate in isolation. They coordinate. A single business objective might involve a chain of Tasks: a lead generation Task feeding a CRM Task, which triggers a pricing optimization Task, followed by an invoicing Task. This choreography happens behind the scenes. The human user defines the goal; the system executes the steps.

Business owners no longer need to manually connect tools, export files, or write rules. They describe what they want to happen—"Launch a promotion and track conversions"—and LIBBi's Task ecosystem makes it happen across departments, tools, and timelines.

Even more powerful is how custom orchestration allows these flows to adapt to unique business processes. Whether a company runs a single-location storefront or a multi-branch enterprise, LIBBi's orchestration engine molds to fit the work—not the other way around.

The result? Human time is preserved for what matters: creative problem-solving, customer relationships, and strategic thinking. AI takes care of the rest.

Preparing for Human+AI Collaboration in Every Role

To thrive in this new environment, businesses must prepare for a reality where AI is no longer just a tool—it is a teammate. As we've seen throughout earlier chapters, particularly in our discussions of trust in Chapter 8 and task orchestration in Chapter 7, the most powerful AI systems are not those that operate in isolation, but those that integrate seamlessly into human workflows. They don't replace human thinking—they amplify it. But this amplification only happens when teams are ready to work with AI, not just around it.

This readiness requires a mindset shift. Thoughtful team members must ask not, "What can AI do for me?" but, "How can I use AI and AI Tasks to become better, faster, and more valuable to my business and team?" In this new model, the standout employees won't be the ones who can do the most manual work—they'll be the ones who know how to orchestrate smart systems, interpret AI-driven insights, and guide machine intelligence toward meaningful outcomes.

For businesses, this means rethinking more than just software deployment. It means redefining culture, retraining teams, and reframing leadership priorities. The old model asked employees to become more efficient executors. The new model demands that they become curators, supervisors, and interpreters of AI-powered processes—people who can delegate with discernment, spot when AI is misfiring, and know when to step in with human context.

This transition demands new competencies: digital fluency, systems thinking, ethical reasoning, and comfort with ambiguity, regardless of industry. It also calls for soft skills—collaboration, creativity, leadership, and resilience—as AI continues to evolve and reshape tasks at a rapid pace. These are not just technical upgrades; they are human upgrades.

It also demands trust—both in the technology and in the teams deploying it. As discussed in Chapter 8, AI that cannot be explained, governed, or aligned with human values will not earn adoption. Businesses must create cultures where employees understand what AI can and cannot do—and where they feel empowered to question, override, or escalate when needed. Delegation to AI must be responsible, not blind.

Some have called this collaboration between human workers and AI "augmented intelligence." The notion is not artificial intelligence that operates independently of human input, but a powerful partnership where machines handle speed, scale, and structure, while humans provide context, judgment, and vision. It's the fusion of machine efficiency with human insight, and it's already reshaping the most forward-thinking organizations.

In their book *Humans + Machines*, Paul Daugherty and H. James Wilson introduce the idea of "fusion skills"—the new capabilities required to thrive in AI-augmented environments. These skills go beyond technical know-how. They include the ability to:

- Understand how algorithms are structured and where their blind spots lie
- Interpret AI outputs in light of business context or customer nuance
- Collaborate with AI agents as dynamic contributors to a shared goal
- Know when to trust automation, when to question it, and when to override it

In other words, fusion skills are not about learning to code—they're about learning to lead in a world where AI is not a back-end system, but a front-line collaborator. They are the skills of orchestration, not just execution; of governance, not just generation.

We are often asked for our view on AI and the workforce due to our involvement in building the first Intelligent Business Management Platform™. We have taken the position that the workforce at large does not need to develop special algorithmic skill sets or develop a masters level knowledge base on prompt engineering, as some would suggest, but that it must keenly understand how to use the best AI powered Tasks at its disposal. If new literacy around intelligent systems is required, where is the thrust of training and leadership? Our belief for most professionals is that it should be placed on how best to leverage the tools – not necessarily how to create them. The thrust is on equipping the organization to work in partnership with intelligent systems, and great systems can make that transition simple and intuitive.

In the intelligent business of the future, every role will involve some form of AI collaboration. Marketing teams will co-write with generative tools. Finance teams will forecast with algorithmic models. Customer service will blend empathy with machine-suggested responses. Even roles in construction, logistics, and field services will use AI to streamline decision-making, reduce waste, and improve outcomes. And, in almost every instance, this collaboration can be supported via a subscribed AI Task. Members of the team, also, become the most powerful designers of AI Tasks as they identify what else they wish it could do – missing Tasks that might further empower the team and workforce. In powerful Intelligent Business Management Platform™ solutions like LIBBi, the workforce can simply request a new task that is promptly built and made available, creating an ongoing positive feedback loop that further powers the collaboration between human and machine. These workers don't need to code the Tasks—they simply define the outcome they want, and the platform facilitates the build process through guided inputs and internal orchestration.

In the late 18th century, as the Industrial Revolution swept through England, one of the most controversial inventions was Richard Arkwright's water frame—an early mechanical spinning machine used to produce cotton thread. When first introduced, the water frame and similar machines were met with fierce resistance. Skilled textile workers feared displacement, and many believed the mechanization of spinning would destroy craftsmanship and livelihoods.

But something different happened. As workers began to learn how to operate, maintain, and eventually improve the machines, they became more than laborers—they became supervisors, technicians, and production planners. Instead of spinning a few threads by hand each day, they oversaw machines that could produce hundreds. Businesses grew, but so did opportunities. Wages rose, factory conditions gradually improved, and the need for skilled machine operators created a new middle tier of industrial employment. Human skill wasn't erased—it was rechanneled into managing, refining, and scaling mechanical power.

That early lesson still applies today: working with the machine does not diminish human value—it multiplies it.

Fast-forward to the 1990s and early 2000s, when the internet reshaped the business world. Many office workers feared that email, search engines, and intranet portals would make administrative roles obsolete. In fact, the opposite occurred. Professionals who embraced digital workflows—who learned how to navigate file-sharing systems, CRM platforms, and cloud-based tools—became more valuable, not less.

Consider the evolution of the marketing department. Once reliant on print ads, physical mailers, and hand-tracked campaigns, marketers who adopted early digital tools gained the ability to target, analyze, and optimize in real-time. They didn't become less creative—they became data-informed creatives. Administrative professionals who once managed calendars and filing cabinets learned to manage entire project workflows across digital teams, scaling their impact and rising into operations roles.

185

The businesses that thrived during the digital transformation weren't the ones who feared the internet—they were the ones that taught their people how to integrate it into everyday work. And the individuals who succeeded weren't those who resisted, but those who asked, *"How can I use this tool to get more done?"*

The question, then, is no longer *whether* this shift is coming. It's already here. The real question is: How well will we prepare our people—not just to survive in this future, but to lead in it? That preparation starts with mindset. It matures through training. And it culminates in a culture where humans and machines are not rivals, but teammates—with each elevating the other.

Final Thoughts: The Future of Work is Not Artificial

Chapter 9 marks a turning point—not just in this book, but in how we think about the nature of work itself. We have traced the arc from historical transformations like the Industrial Revolution to the modern evolution of digital and AI-powered workflows. We have seen how the integration of AI into business processes is not a threat to human value, but a powerful invitation to elevate it. We've explored how intelligent systems can liberate professionals from repetitive execution and empower them to focus on creativity, judgment, and leadership.

This chapter also reframes what it means to prepare a workforce—not by making everyone a technologist, but by ensuring every team member knows how to work *with* intelligent tools. The skills of the future are fusion skills: the ability to delegate wisely, interpret critically, and guide AI to meaningful business outcomes. As we look ahead, it becomes clear that AI is not replacing work—it is redefining it. And the businesses that thrive will be those that view this not as disruption, but as an opportunity to orchestrate

186

better systems, smarter teams, and more impactful results.

Part IV is about leadership, transformation, and adaptation. Chapter 10 will take us deeper into how organizations can build an AI-augmented workforce—not just through tools, but through roles, values, and culture. The future of work isn't artificial. It's intelligent, it's collaborative, and it's already unfolding around us. Now, it's time to lead within it.

This is not about someday. It's about right now. The workforce is already changing. The only question is whether your business is changing with it.

In the chapters ahead, we'll explore what it means to lead an AI-augmented workforce, how to build a culture that thrives alongside intelligent systems, and how to ensure that the rise of automation also elevates the human role in business—not just replaces it.

The future of work is not artificial.

It's augmented. It's orchestrated. And it's already here.

Chapter 10: Building the AI-Augmented Workforce

In Chapter 9, we explored how the nature of work is evolving—from hands-on execution to strategic oversight, from doing tasks to directing intelligent systems. We looked at how AI is repositioning human effort away from repetitive functions and toward higher-order thinking, coordination, and decision-making. We also reflected on history—on Richard Arkwright's water frame and the digital revolution of the 1990s—both reminders that when workers embrace new tools, they aren't replaced. They're elevated.

That same opportunity stands before us now. But to fully realize it, we must shift our lens—from the nature of work to the people doing it.

This chapter turns the focus to the workforce itself: the roles, mindsets, skills, and systems that will shape success in the age of intelligent business. We'll explore how organizations can build cultures of AI collaboration, how talent can be upskilled and redeployed, how new workforce models—like task-based support networks—can address capability gaps while opening doors for displaced or underutilized workers, and why ethics in AI isn't just a technical requirement, but a cultural one.

Chapter 10 presents a fundamental question: How do we prepare today's workforce not only to *adapt* to AI—but to *lead* within it?

Redefining Roles: Task Generalists, Specialists, and Professionals

The AI-augmented workforce will not be one-size-fits-all. It will be layered, flexible, and shaped around how people work with systems. As explored earlier, the collaboration between humans and intelligent platforms is not a story of replacement—it is a model of enhancement. AI Tasks allow employees to move from repetitive execution to strategic oversight. Rather than reduce the value of the workforce, these tools amplify it, enabling employees to make more meaningful contributions while freeing them from manual bottlenecks. This human-AI partnership leads to elevated performance, greater job satisfaction, and a more agile organization.

As businesses adopt more AI-powered workflows, they will inevitably encounter both new opportunities and unexpected needs. Some will discover gaps that require specialized expertise—support in deploying AI tools, guidance in activating intelligent systems, or access to professionals fluent in AI Task implementation. Others may find that while automation reduces the demand for certain full-time roles, it doesn't eliminate the need for targeted, high-skill support in specific areas.

We've already explored how AI is likely to reshape the workforce— potentially leading to net reductions in certain professions, particularly where repetitive tasks dominate. But for the purposes of this chapter, it's enough to acknowledge a simple—and perhaps understated—truth: the needs of businesses will shift, often unpredictably, as AI becomes more integrated and continues to evolve.

And this shift creates a new kind of opportunity.

What emerges is the rise of a certified, on-demand freelance workforce— ready to step in and support businesses with the precision, flexibility, and AI fluency this new environment demands. In Chapter 7, we explored how freelance developers are building and monetizing AI Tasks within a growing digital ecosystem. That same model—the autonomy, adaptability, and direct-to-need engagement—can also be applied to a broader range of professional services.

The same forces driving the rise of the freelance developer are now creating space for a new kind of AI-literate professional: individuals who offer support, strategy, training, and task execution on demand. Not as permanent employees—but as agile partners in an intelligent, rapidly evolving business landscape.

Imagine a marketplace of trained professionals available to support businesses on-demand—customer service experts certified in Task deployment, marketers who specialize in using AI to drive campaign outcomes, or HR professionals who know how to implement compliance-driven onboarding Tasks. These individuals aren't general freelancers—they can be system-ready, certified contributors who can plug into a business and add value immediately. This creates a powerful win-win: businesses gain access to precise, scalable talent, and freelancers gain access to a robust pipeline of meaningful work.

As an example, we built this functionality into our solution, LIBBi. The model provides defined freelance roles for the AI-augmented workforce. Task Generalists and Task Specialists.

To more specifically define:

- Task Generalists: These cross-functional contributors are AI-savvy operators who can quickly implement Tasks across multiple departments. For example, a Task Generalist could help a small business owner configure and deploy a suite of foundational Tasks: customer intake, appointment scheduling, invoice generation, and follow-up messaging. Within a single afternoon, they could activate these capabilities inside the business, creating a seamless front-office workflow that reduces administrative time by 60% or more. For businesses that lack the bandwidth or know-how to implement digital tools on their own, access to a Generalist for just a few hours can turn "we should automate this" into "this is now automated."

- Task Specialists: These are domain-specific experts—such as digital marketers, HR leads, or financial analysts—who know both the business function and the best AI Tasks to support it. Imagine a Task Specialist in marketing brought in by a home services business. Over the course of a 3-hour engagement, they activate a Task that generates segmented customer outreach campaigns, integrates AI-generated content with the company's promotions calendar, and sets up analytics tracking on campaign performance. What might have taken a team a full week—or required outsourcing to a digital agency—can now be completed in an afternoon with sharper targeting and faster insights. For the business, the combination of expertise and AI precision is a strategic edge that compounds over time.

The real value of these roles is in how they operate in practice. With just a few hours of support from a certified contributor—combined with the activation of exactly the right AI Task—businesses can unlock efficiency, insight, and strategy that would otherwise take days or even weeks to achieve. Each of these roles is not just supported—they are certified, trained, and tracked through performance feedback loops.

To better illustrate how businesses might practically leverage this model, we share a hypothetical company that has chosen to implement the LIBBi platform.

FreshCoat Painting, a residential and light commercial painting company based in Nashville, had built its reputation on quality craftsmanship and reliable service. The business, led by owner Maya, had grown steadily over time through referrals and word-of-mouth. But when Maya began planning to expand into two neighboring counties, it became clear that the business's internal systems weren't equipped to scale.

Key operational processes—like job scheduling, estimating, and invoicing—were still handled manually. Scheduling happened via text messages and spreadsheets. Estimates were handwritten. Invoices were often delayed, and payment tracking required constant follow-up. Marketing efforts were inconsistent and often reactive, rather than strategic.

Recognizing that these inefficiencies would limit growth, Maya decided to implement the Intelligent Business Management Platform™ solution, LIBBi. With no in-house IT support and limited bandwidth to configure the system herself, she opted to bring in outside help to accelerate adoption.

Through the platform's built-in support interface, Maya hired a Task Generalist—a certified freelancer trained to deploy automation tools across small business operations. With immediate access to her environment (thanks to structured access controls within the platform), the Generalist began implementing foundational workflows.

Within a few hours, FreshCoat's inquiry process was automated: new website submissions triggered a Job Intake Task, customer scheduling was handled by an AI-powered calendar, and estimates could be generated using a standardized Estimate Generator Task. Payment delays were resolved through automated Invoicing and Payment Tasks, which streamlined billing and reminders. For Maya, these improvements significantly reduced the time spent on administrative tasks and freed her to focus on growth.

Next, Maya sought to improve marketing performance. She engaged a Marketing Task Specialist—another certified freelancer with expertise in campaign strategy and experience deploying AI-driven tools through the platform. The Specialist worked inside Maya's workspace, leveraging customer data to identify high-value client segments, launching targeted email and SMS campaigns using a Campaign Builder Task, and configuring a Social Media Posting Task to automate weekly job highlights.

They also implemented a Lead Scoring Task, which helped prioritize incoming inquiries based on historical patterns, enabling Maya to respond quickly to the most promising leads. Within a week of launching the campaign, FreshCoat booked several new jobs—some of which included upsells based on AI-generated service suggestions.

Notably, none of these professionals were added to Maya's staff. They required no formal onboarding, no long-term contracts, and no direct access to sensitive systems outside the structured platform. Their work was delivered through modular engagements, driven by clear objectives and enabled by platform-native controls.

For FreshCoat Painting, the results were twofold: a more efficient operation and a more strategic approach to growth. But perhaps more importantly, the case illustrates a broader trend—how small businesses can remain agile and competitive by accessing specialized talent exactly when and where it's needed, without overextending internal capacity.

This shift—from full-time staffing to on-demand, AI-enabled support—is one example of how intelligent workforce models are reshaping how modern businesses scale.

These roles—Task Generalists and Task Specialists—are not abstract constructs. They are practical solutions to real-world business needs. As companies begin implementing and expanding their intelligent infrastructure, these professionals become essential extensions of the internal team. Whether supporting everyday workflows or helping launch strategic initiatives, they provide a flexible, efficient way to get the right expertise exactly when it's needed.

Workforce Certification and Upskilling-as-a-Service

In an era where intelligent systems are transforming operations at every level, the most successful organizations understand a key truth: sustainable transformation doesn't begin with technology. It begins with people.

Companies navigating digital and AI transitions are discovering that their greatest asset isn't the software they adopt—it's the workforce they develop. Teams that thrive in this environment aren't just using smarter tools. They're being equipped with the skills, confidence, and strategic insight to lead change from within. The companies getting this right are building learning into the fabric of work—not as a side initiative, but as a continuous, embedded function of daily operations.

This requires a new approach to workforce development—one built on contextual learning, role-based fluency, and accessible certification. Traditional training models—detached from the tools themselves and delivered in abstract settings—are no longer enough. In contrast, leading organizations are investing in upskilling models that align directly with how employees work. Micro-certifications tied to specific systems and functions are replacing broad credentials. Real-time learning, delivered inside the task flow, is replacing one-size-fits-all training.

Take Amazon's Career Choice program as one example. Rather than viewing upskilling as a way to serve internal job pipelines exclusively, Amazon offered workers access to high-demand training in areas like logistics, cloud computing, and data analytics—even if that training led them outside the company. This expansive view of workforce investment paid dividends—not just in skill acquisition, but in employee engagement, internal mobility, and reputation. The program recognized a vital point: long-term competitiveness doesn't come from automating people out. It comes from equipping them to evolve with the work.

Similarly, PwC's Digital Accelerator Program reimagined employees not as passive recipients of change, but as drivers of it. Rather than hiring externally to meet new digital demands, PwC invested in its internal consultants—training them in AI, automation, and analytics, then redeploying them as transformation leaders across the business. These individuals didn't just improve process efficiency—they influenced team culture, accelerated adoption, and became internal multipliers of innovation.

IBM's SkillsBuild initiative extended this logic even further—providing structured AI and cloud training not just to employees, but to underserved communities, external learners, and nonprofit partners. It wasn't just a technical training platform—it was a statement of values. By combining accessibility with ethical alignment, IBM demonstrated that responsible AI transformation begins with how a company chooses to educate and empower others.

These examples point toward a new model of workforce readiness—one where upskilling is:

- Role-based and relevant to real tasks

- Modular and measurable, with micro-certifications that track actual fluency

- Peer-supported, with access to coaches, colleagues, and professionals who reinforce learning in the moment

This shift is also reflected in thought leadership. Darrell M. West, in *The Future of Work*, argues that AI and automation will fundamentally redefine job paths—and that dynamic, lifelong learning ecosystems will be essential to maintaining both workforce security and enterprise performance. In *AI in Business*, John Smith emphasizes the role of internal learning cultures, where curiosity, experimentation, and shared knowledge replace rigid hierarchies. Both perspectives converge on the same idea: organizations that learn faster, adapt faster.

Across industries, the movement is clear. Companies are shifting from static roles to fluid, skills-based models. Teams are being reorganized not by job title, but by capability. And learning is no longer something that happens before the work—but as part of it.

In this environment, AI should not be viewed as a replacement for human talent. It should be seen as a catalyst for human growth. The organizations that understand this—that embed upskilling into their systems, align training to real-world outputs, and reward adaptability over legacy credentials—will be the ones that build not just stronger operations, but stronger people.

Of course, workforce upscaling is also achievable through deployment of freelance talent, such as the Task Generalist and Task Specialists roles discussed earlier. In the case of the LIBBi Task Workforce, for example, professionals who are engaged in these roles are both highly trained and certified. Ultimately, where human intelligence is a major differentiator of business success, investment in training and certification is not only prudent, but essential.

Cross-Functional Collaboration Through AI Orchestration

The AI-Augmented Workforce doesn't just work smarter—it works together. As businesses grow more complex, so too does the need for speed, alignment, and seamless coordination across departments. Historically, organizations have relied on departmental silos—each with its own tools, data, and processes—to manage daily operations. But the future of intelligent work demands more than localized efficiency. It demands cross-functional orchestration, where every part of the business communicates and executes in synchrony.

We offer our LIBBi solution as an example of how synchronization works in practice. In LIBBi, this orchestration happens at the Task level. AI-powered Tasks trigger, sequence, and manage workflows across departments, turning fragmented processes into end-to-end operational flows. A marketing specialist might launch a promotional campaign that automatically initiates a Finance Forecasting Task, which then prompts an Operations Task to adjust staffing or inventory. Each of these steps is powered by AI, but guided by human intention—giving professionals control while accelerating throughput.

This type of integration once required custom-coded workflows, middleware, or expensive project management software. But in an AI-native solution, departments no longer need to translate their needs into IT tickets or depend on disconnected tools. Instead, they operate in a shared language of Tasks. Users initiate actions with intuitive prompts. AI interprets the business objective, coordinates with relevant processes, and executes across the organization—accurately, consistently, and with full transparency.

This isn't theoretical. It's already reshaping competitive advantage in other solutions, as well. Consider Slack, which uses AI and automation to trigger cross-departmental workflows directly within collaborative threads. A support ticket can initiate follow-up tasks in product and sales, all without leaving the conversation. Similarly, Asana has built intelligent routing that allows task completion in one department to automatically trigger project updates, budget allocations, or resourcing changes in others. These platforms deliver intelligent coordination as a core function of everyday work.

Effective workflow orchestration hinges on more than just automation—it also requires systems that are accessible, modular, and context-aware. In many organizations, siloed tools, conflicting data sets, and manual handoffs continue to limit operational coherence. The goal of orchestration is to break those silos, creating workflows where tasks across departments can operate in sequence, informed by shared context and responsive to real-time conditions.

A modular task framework allows for this kind of coordination without requiring heavy engineering or custom integration. When each task feeds into a secure, centralized data structure, departments can operate with a consistent understanding of the business state—eliminating redundant entry, communication gaps, and version conflicts.

Here's what such orchestration might look like in practice:

- A Customer Feedback Task collects post-service responses and, if ratings fall below a set threshold, automatically triggers a Compliance Review Task for further analysis.

- A Revenue Monitoring Task detects a significant sales uptick and initiates an HR Task to assess staffing needs and begin a targeted hiring process before strain appears.

- A Job Completion Task from a field team sets off a chain: first, a Customer Notification Task sends an update, followed by a Billing Task that finalizes invoicing—no interdepartmental handoff required.

These are not isolated automations—they represent coordinated sequences that reflect operational priorities. When done well, this kind of orchestration creates a rhythm across departments, aligning teams around shared goals while reducing friction.

But the success of such systems doesn't rest solely on technical capability. It also depends on how people interact with the tools. The most effective platforms give users agency—allowing them to adjust workflows, configure task logic, and determine which actions require human judgment. This balance between automation and control fosters a stronger relationship between people and systems.

Daniel H. Pink's framework in *Drive* is particularly relevant here. He identifies three elements that fuel motivation in modern work: autonomy, mastery, and purpose. In orchestrated systems, users experience all three. They have autonomy in how workflows are configured and adjusted. They gain mastery as they become fluent in using and refining these tools. And they see purpose when every task they execute contributes to broader organizational objectives—whether that's customer satisfaction, operational efficiency, or business growth.

In such environments, automation isn't a replacement for human input—it's a structure that elevates it. Users aren't passive recipients of predefined processes; they are contributors to an evolving operational system. They guide when to intervene, shape how tasks unfold, and identify where improvements can be made.

Ultimately, this is what orchestration at scale enables: not just departments doing more, but organizations moving more coherently—where systems respond to the business in real time, and people are empowered to shape how work gets done.

Building Talent Pipelines for AI-Era Roles

As technology continues to reshape the nature of work, a key question is emerging across industries: *Are we building the right talent pipelines—not just for today's demands, but for tomorrow's capabilities?* The rise of AI in business isn't just creating new tools; it's redefining the skills and mindsets that matter most. And in this new landscape, the organizations that adapt fastest aren't necessarily those that hire the most technical talent—they're the ones that invest in cultivating it from within.

Traditional approaches to talent development—focused on fixed roles and formal credentials—are increasingly misaligned with the needs of intelligent systems. Today's most valuable team members aren't always the ones with the longest résumés. Instead, they are those who:

- Learn new tools quickly and independently

- Recognize patterns and opportunities for automation

- Contribute to the refinement or deployment of AI-powered workflows

- Demonstrate adaptability across departments and systems

In this context, talent is no longer a static asset acquired through recruitment. It's a dynamic capability that organizations must nurture, support, and evolve.

Modern AI business systems can help facilitate this evolution. By capturing how employees interact with Tasks—how they configure, adjust, and scale them—organizations gain insight into who is becoming fluent in intelligent collaboration. This data isn't just operational—it becomes developmental. A frontline worker who modifies a scheduling Task to better reflect real-time demand is demonstrating both initiative and systems thinking. A generalist who improves how CRM data feeds into reporting Tasks is effectively bridging the gap between customer experience and decision-making.

These examples are more than operational wins—they represent a shift in how value is created inside organizations. Skill development is no longer confined to formal training programs; it happens in real time, through active engagement with the systems that power the business.

Contrast this with companies that failed to evolve. Kodak is a well-documented example. Once a market leader in photography, Kodak held early patents and insights into digital imaging—and even explored AI-assisted imaging capabilities. But it failed to build the internal momentum needed to shift its business. Instead of reskilling its workforce to support a digital future, Kodak remained anchored to its legacy film operations. While competitors like Canon, Nikon, and later Apple invested in new technologies and retrained their teams to support them, Kodak's talent strategy stayed fixed. The company lacked not only the tools, but the organizational agility to respond—and in 2012, it declared bankruptcy.

Kodak's story is a cautionary one, but not unique. As intelligent technologies continue to move from the edge of operations to the center, businesses that do not evolve their workforce strategies risk misalignment between capability and opportunity.

The alternative is clear. The most resilient organizations will treat talent development not as an HR function, but as a core component of strategic execution. They will build systems that:

- Identify emerging skill sets in real time

- Provide flexible, task-based opportunities for learning

- Reward adaptability and initiative, not just experience

- View every interaction with technology as a learning moment

In the age of AI, success won't come from hiring the most technically advanced workforce—it will come from developing a workforce that grows

alongside the technology. Organizations that embrace this will not only keep pace with change—they'll help shape it.

AI as a Reflection of Human Principles

Artificial intelligence does not create values—it reflects them. The systems we design, the data we train them on, and the permissions we embed are all outcomes of human decisions. These choices are never neutral. They are shaped by organizational priorities, ethical frameworks, operational assumptions, and cultural norms. As businesses adopt AI, they aren't merely automating processes—they are encoding decision-making structures that carry implicit (and sometimes explicit) expressions of what the organization believes.

Each time a team defines how a system should respond to a customer complaint, determines what thresholds should trigger a human review, or decides which workflows remain manual, they are shaping the character of their organization in code. In this way, AI becomes more than a tool—it becomes a mirror. It reflects how an organization interprets risk, fairness, speed, accountability, and customer care.

This makes leadership in the AI era fundamentally different. As discussed in Chapter 1, the use of AI is not simply a technical deployment—it's a form of governance. Leaders are accountable not only for the outcomes produced by their systems, but for the design logic behind them. As intelligent platforms become embedded into daily operations, the line between strategic intent and technical configuration begins to blur. System behavior becomes organizational behavior.

Consider a scenario in which a business configures escalation rules, access levels, and review protocols in an AI-driven task management system. These decisions—whether to prioritize responsiveness over caution, to decentralize decision-making or retain control—encode deeper institutional beliefs. Automation becomes a means of formalizing culture: not just how work gets done, but *how it should get done.*

In this environment, intelligence is not centralized in a single department or executive layer. It is distributed—accessible to frontline staff and cross-functional teams who can initiate tasks, interpret outputs, and propose refinements. Task feedback loops feed directly into strategic dashboards, connecting day-to-day activity with higher-level goals. And as machine efficiency scales, the value of human judgment becomes more—not less—essential. The relationship between automation and insight becomes complementary, not competitive.

This shift aligns with the framework put forth in *Rewired* by Eric Lamarre and Kate Smaje. The authors argue that digital transformation is rarely about implementing new technology alone. It requires rethinking how decisions are made, how accountability is shared, and how value is generated throughout the organization. Technology, in their view, becomes transformational only when it is integrated into the cultural and operational routines of the business.

Embedding AI in this way requires more than functional deployment—it requires structural intention. When companies design systems that reflect their values and distribute responsibility intelligently, they don't just accelerate output. They reinforce who they are. And in doing so, they increase trust—both inside and outside the organization.

Ultimately, intelligent work will not be defined by systems that replace people, but by systems that scale human judgment, creativity, and principle. AI will not determine what matters. It will reveal what already does. The organizations that succeed in this next era will not be those with the most sophisticated technology—but those with the clearest sense of what they want that technology to represent.

Final Thoughts: The Intelligent Workforce

The future of work isn't just more automated—it's more human-centered, more cross-functional, and more intentionally designed. What we've explored in this chapter and throughout Part IV is not a distant vision or theoretical framework—it's an emerging reality already taking shape inside forward-thinking organizations.

We've seen how redefining workforce roles, orchestrating AI-driven workflows, and embedding ethical considerations into system design can elevate—not replace—the people at the heart of the business. The companies best positioned to succeed aren't necessarily those with the most advanced technology. They're the ones that empower their teams to work *with* it—confidently, creatively, and purposefully.

Satya Nadella captured this shift when he said, "In the future, every employee will be expected to work with AI like they work with email today." That future isn't approaching—it's already underway. AI fluency is becoming a baseline requirement, not a specialized skill. But recognizing that isn't enough. The organizations that will truly lead are those that commit to continuous reinvention—not just of their tools, but of their workforce model.

As Ginni Rometty observed, "The era of 'learn and earn' is replacing the old model of 'learn, work, retire.'" That shift is central to the intelligent workforce. It reframes learning as a lifelong, embedded component of work itself—where growth is not a separate track, but part of every task, every role, and every interaction.

Part of this evolution involves rethinking how businesses access support. As teams become leaner, more flexible, and more focused on high-value outcomes, the need for supplemental talent grows. Not every organization has the in-house expertise—or the bandwidth—to implement AI-powered solutions or manage complex workflows alone. That's where the Task Workforce becomes essential.

The Task Workforce introduces new roles—such as Task Generalists and Task Specialists—trained professionals who can be engaged on-demand to help deploy, manage, and optimize intelligent business systems. Whether a company is adjusting its workforce model, needs short-term support, or wants to add new capabilities without committing to permanent hires, these roles offer a flexible, cost-effective path to progress. They provide targeted help precisely when and where it's needed, bridging the gap between vision and execution.

Real-world examples have made this tangible. Companies like Amazon, PwC, and IBM didn't wait for disruption to force change. They invested early in their people—building internal ecosystems of training, upskilling, and AI collaboration that turned their workforces into transformation agents. They understood that long-term competitiveness is rooted not just in systems capability, but in human adaptability.

What Part IV reveals is the central tension—and opportunity—of the AI era: how to build intelligent systems without losing the intelligence, creativity, and culture of the people who operate them. It's a leadership challenge. A cultural challenge. And, increasingly, a systems design challenge.

In Part V, we'll shift from vision to execution—from designing intelligent systems to operationalizing them at scale. You'll learn how to assess your organization's readiness, avoid common pitfalls, and build sustained momentum. Because in a world shaped by rapid technological change, leadership is no longer about controlling the outcome. It's about guiding the process—with clarity, with trust, and with a deep commitment to what makes your business *worth* scaling.

Let's get to work.

Chapter 11: Make the Move to AI Playbook

Part IV of this book explored one of the most profound shifts in modern business: the changing nature of work in the age of artificial intelligence. We examined how traditional roles are giving way to more dynamic, task-driven models—and how intelligent systems are not replacing people, but elevating them, embedding support and strategy into the flow of everyday operations.

But now, we turn the page.

If Part IV was about *designing* the intelligent workforce, then Part V is about *activating* it. This is where architecture meets execution—where theory is tested by real business conditions. It's one thing to understand the future of work. It's another to build it.

Chapter 11 is your playbook. It translates strategy into momentum—vision into a structured, actionable plan. There's a well-worn adage that says, "If you don't know where you're going, any road will take you there." This chapter ensures you don't leave with just inspiration—you leave with direction. Whether you're building from scratch or adapting existing systems, you'll come away with the tools to chart a path forward into the age of intelligent business.

To that end, we'll reference our own journey—using LIBBi, the Intelligent Business Management Platform™, as a case study. Not to market, but to illustrate. Our aim is to share what we've learned in building, deploying, and operating an AI-powered system in the real world. But the frameworks we explore here apply broadly—regardless of whether you use LIBBi, another platform, or a custom-built solution that aligns with your specific needs.

You'll learn how to evaluate your organization's readiness for AI adoption, how to launch intelligent workflows without introducing unnecessary friction, and how to avoid the structural missteps that can stall progress before it begins.

As Jason L. Anderson notes in *Artificial Intelligence for Business*, true success with AI doesn't come from the technology alone—it comes from aligning people, processes, and systems around clear objectives. It comes from understanding that transformation isn't just technical. It's cultural. Strategic. Personal.

This chapter is about that alignment. It's about what happens when you stop planning for change—and start running toward it. And, here, we fully deliver on our promise to help you go from uncertainty to action!

Make the Move to AI: Your Business Playbook

Translating strategy into execution requires more than vision—it requires structure, clarity, and a plan you can act on. To support that process, we've developed a guided thought exercise called *Make the Move to AI*—a practical tool designed to help you begin shaping your business playbook for the AI era.

This isn't a generic checklist. It's a structured framework built to help you think critically about your workflows, your data environment, your team structure, and your strategic priorities. Whether you're considering a full Intelligent Business Management Platform™ or exploring other AI-enabled solutions, this exercise is designed to help you approach the transition with clarity.

In the appendix, you'll find the *Make the Move to AI Playbook*—a step-by-step planning guide that mirrors the themes of this chapter. It walks you through the core components of intelligent business implementation: from identifying high-impact workflows and assessing data readiness, to piloting your first Tasks and engaging the right people at the right time. It's not just a readiness assessment—it's a blueprint for operational alignment in an AI-driven world.

You'll also find a digital version of the playbook available through our publisher at www.intelligentpress.co, should you prefer to work through it interactively or share it with your team.

To begin, we invite you to explore the nine foundational questions that follow. Each one is paired with a short reflection and a reference section in the playbook. You can work through them in sequence or take time with each individually. If you're ready, start filling out the playbook now. If not, simply sit with the questions. The value is in the process—because readiness is built through reflection, not rushed decisions.

This is where strategic planning meets operational possibility. Let's begin.

Make the Move to AI Thought Questions:

1. What are your core workflows—and which ones should be automated first?

The first step in building your AI-powered business playbook is to take inventory of the workflows that keep your business running. These may include things like customer onboarding, project tracking, invoicing, or marketing execution. In the *Make the Move to AI* playbook, you'll rate each process based on two key criteria:

- Difficulty to use today (1 = seamless, 5 = frustrating)

- Importance to scale tomorrow (1 = nice to have, 5 = mission-critical)

This dual scoring system helps you cut through the noise and prioritize automation and orchestration where it matters most. You'll quickly see which processes are ripe for transformation—and which can wait. It also gives you a clearer understanding of where AI Tasks will deliver the most immediate impact, streamlining complex work, removing friction, and freeing up your team for more strategic contributions.

Why this Matters:

The difference between AI experimentation and AI transformation lies in *repeatability*. Automating a single process is useful—but building repeatable, cross-functional systems that can scale with your business is what delivers lasting value. Focusing on your core workflows allows you to identify patterns, reduce friction, and build consistency across departments.

When processes are clearly defined and thoughtfully prioritized, it becomes easier to integrate AI tools in ways that align with both current operations and future goals. Repeatable systems not only reduce human error—they also create structure for growth, enabling teams to focus less on managing work and more on directing outcomes.

As Ben Horowitz notes in *The Hard Thing About Hard Things*, when business gets messy, process wins. That's especially true in the age of AI. Successful implementation isn't about automating everything—it's about identifying the right places to start, building intelligently, and creating systems that evolve alongside your business. Starting with

2. What experience do you want to deliver to customers, employees, and partners?

This step invites you to envision your business not just as a set of services—but as a connected, intelligent experience. Whether you're serving external customers, internal teams, or trusted partners, the experience you deliver—online and in-platform—is now a competitive differentiator. In this section of the playbook, you'll define the capabilities you want stakeholders to have at their fingertips. Can customers self-book and pay? Can team members track project updates or trigger follow-ups with ease? Can partners share compliance docs or receive updates automatically?

Why this matters:

As business leaders, one of our most important responsibilities is to create experiences that are not only functional—but compelling. A clear vision for your AI-powered interaction model allows you to translate values into action—offering stakeholders convenience, transparency, and confidence in every touchpoint. The danger is falling into "shiny object syndrome"—deploying flashy AI features or fragmented tools that solve surface-level problems without delivering lasting value or coherence. This step grounds you in what actually matters to your users, so that every Task, workflow, and automation drives meaningful engagement.

Take Chick-fil-A as an example. While known for its in-person service, the company has built a seamless digital ordering, loyalty, and operations platform that makes it easy for customers to order, customize, track, and pay—whether on mobile or in-store. Behind the scenes, their employees also use AI-driven systems for kitchen routing, scheduling, and inventory. The experience is deliberately orchestrated, not just functional—and that clarity has been a major driver of their operational efficiency, customer satisfaction, and continued market share growth.

As an example, our solution LIBBi enables this kind of orchestrated experience—but it remains vital that you first decide what kind of experience you want to lead with. This section of the playbook is your opportunity to shape that vision—clearly, intentionally, and with the flexibility to evolve as your business grows.

3. Where is your data currently stored—and is it secure and centralized?

This section challenges you to take inventory of where your business-critical data actually lives today. Is it in spreadsheets on personal laptops? Scattered across Dropbox, Google Drive, and iCloud? Buried in email threads or siloed within a CRM or accounting platform? Chances are, your data is more fragmented than you think.

You'll also assess whether your data is secure, up to date, and accessible by the right people at the right time.

Why this matters:

Disconnected or insecure data is the single biggest blocker to effective AI implementation and one of the easiest to solve with the right tools. AI doesn't just need access to data—it needs trusted, real-time, structured data that can be orchestrated across your business. As an example, we built our solution LIBBi i to eliminate fragmentation by creating a centralized, secure data layer that all Tasks can access and update.

When your data is unified, each Task you deploy—whether for onboarding, service fulfillment, billing, or analytics—contributes to a living system of insight and action. They are orchestrated agents that talk to each other, learn from each other, and compound each other's value. As Max Bennett writes in *A Brief History of Intelligence*, true intelligence doesn't live in isolated functions—it emerges from connectivity and shared context.

As discussed in Chapter 8, data fragmentation quietly erodes performance, inflates costs, and causes teams to second-guess decisions. Reconciliation becomes constant. Reports don't align. Teams operate on outdated or incomplete information.

LIBBi solves this by becoming your single source of operational truth. Every Task runs off the same data. Every department pulls from the same playbook. And every decision becomes more confident, more timely, and more consistent. And, as you use the platform, your data set and insight about your business grows.

By understanding where your data lives today—and whether it's ready to fuel intelligent workflows—you'll take one of the most important steps toward building an AI-enabled business that thinks clearly and moves fast.

4. Who needs to be involved in this transformation?

AI may power your workflows, but it's people who drive the transformation. In this step, you'll identify the team members, department leads, collaborators, or external advisors who should be part of planning, implementing, and leading your move to AI.

Don't just think about your tech team—include stakeholders from every corner of your organization: operations, finance, sales, customer experience, marketing, compliance, and more. This is about bringing together the voices and knowledge that understand your workflows, own your data, and influence your culture.

Why this matters:

AI may enable the systems—but people will be a central element to shaping the outcomes. The success or failure of any AI initiative depends both on the tools you choose and on the people you engage. Too often, technology decisions are made in isolation—led by a small group, without input from the teams most affected. The result? Misalignment, resistance, and lost momentum.

Involving the right individuals early—those who understand your workflows, manage your data, and influence your culture—creates shared ownership, remember this concept from Chapter 1. It ensures that implementation is grounded in real operational needs, not abstract plans. It also uncovers gaps, surface concerns, and opens space for honest conversations about change.

This question isn't just about logistics—it's about leadership. The people you invite into this process will shape how your organization experiences AI: as a burden or an opportunity, as an external pressure or a shared evolution. Inclusion isn't just good practice—it's advance preparation for adoption.

As we'll explore in Chapter 12, transformation is rarely blocked by a lack of tools. It's blocked by a lack of trust. And trust is built when leaders communicate early, include the right voices, and frame change as something the organization does *together*. The real challenge isn't just selecting the right system. It's choosing the right people to help shape it, guide it, and make it meaningful. Because in the end, the most powerful force behind any AI transformation isn't the code. It's the culture.

5. What platforms are you already paying for?

This step is your opportunity to inventory all of the SaaS platforms your business currently uses—from CRMs and marketing automation tools to payment processors, email systems, and task management apps. For each, list the estimated monthly cost and the core function it serves.

You might be surprised by how many tools your business has accumulated—and how few of them are fully integrated, consistently used, or cost-efficient.

Why this matters:

Most businesses are overpaying for overlapping software. As your tech stack grows, so does your operational friction: duplicate data, redundant workflows, disconnected teams, and compounding costs.

Let's look at a realistic example.

A 25-person professional services business might be paying for the following:

• CRM (HubSpot) – $800/month

• Marketing Automation (ActiveCampaign) – $500/month

• Accounting Software (QuickBooks Online Advanced) – $180/month

• Financial Reporting Tool (Fathom or Spotlight Reporting) – $200/month

- Large Language Model or AI Assistant Subscription – $99/month

- Email Platform (Google Workspace for Business) – $300/month

- API Automation Tool (Zapier or Make) – $150/month

- Scheduling Tool (Calendly Pro or Acuity) – $120/month

- Proposal/Bid Platform (PandaDoc, Proposify) – $150/month

- Form Builder (Typeform, Jotform) – $70/month

- Customer Support (Zendesk or Help Scout) – $250/month

- Project Management (Asana, Trello Premium) – $250/month

- Client Portal Software (SuiteDash, Clinked) – $300/month

Total: ~$3,369/month ($40,000+ per year)

And that doesn't include training, integrations, or tool fatigue.

It is possible to replace 70% or more of this "stack" with a single, unified system—one login, one data layer, and one integrated workflow hub.

This section of the playbook isn't just about budgeting—it's about identifying the inefficiencies that slow you down and asking:

What could we do if we didn't have to duct-tape our business together?

6. Which business policies do you need to adopt or update?

As you deploy an Intelligent Business Management Platform™ like LIBBi or other solution you choose, you're not just transforming workflows—you're rethinking how your business operates, governs, and communicates its values. This step invites you to evaluate which foundational policies your business already has, which are outdated, and which should be adopted or refined for an AI-powered future.

You'll reflect on key operational policies such as privacy, terms of service, GDPR compliance, cookie usage, and—importantly—AI transparency and ethical use. These aren't just check-the-box legal requirements. They are how you define your company's contract with its customers, employees, partners, and regulators.

Why this matters:

In Chapter 2, we explored the evolving ethics of AI—how intelligent systems are no longer just code, but reflections of the values of those who build and deploy them. In that chapter, we made the case that leadership in the AI era is inseparable from ethical foresight. Now, in this chapter, we apply that lesson directly to your business infrastructure.

Policies are the tangible expression of that foresight. They show how your business handles data, respects consent, defines accountability, and navigates complexity. AI doesn't just need performance—it needs principles. And those principles must be written, communicated, and enforced clearly.

But beyond compliance, this is an opportunity to lead. A thoughtfully written privacy policy or AI use disclosure isn't just a legal shield—it's a message to your stakeholders that says: *We take your trust seriously. We've thought this through.*

As we noted in Chapter 2, AI will scale whatever we design—our priorities, our principles, our blind spots. Updating your policies ensures that what gets scaled is aligned with who you are and where you're going.

Because in an intelligent, automated business, your policies are more than just paperwork. They're architecture. They're leadership. And they're the foundation for building systems—and relationships—that endure.

7. What additional support do you need?

AI transformation is not a solo sport. It requires smart planning, thoughtful execution, and the right people—at the right time—to bring it all together. This section invites you to reflect on where your business could benefit from expert support.

Do you need help mapping your data to your workflows? That's where a Task Generalist comes in.

Do you need help deploying AI for marketing, HR, finance, or compliance? That's where a Task Specialist can step in with targeted insight.

Why this matters:

As explored in Chapter 10, the workforce is evolving beyond traditional roles and permanent staffing models. Today, flexibility and access to specialized talent are critical to momentum. The rise of task-based labor—structured around Generalists and Specialists—gives businesses a new way to respond to complexity without overextending internal teams.

A practical example of this is the LIBBi Task Workforce, a certified network of freelance professionals trained to support AI-enabled operations. These individuals can be deployed quickly—without long-term contracts—to assist with implementation, optimization, and training. While every organization will choose the support structure that fits its needs, LIBBi's model reflects a growing trend: building scalable, on-demand access to expertise that complements internal capabilities.

This shift calls for a change in mindset. Instead of asking, *Should we hire someone for this?* leaders are increasingly asking, *Who can help us make meaningful progress this week?*

Before defaulting to doing everything in-house, consider:

- Where could a Generalist provide cross-functional momentum?

- What parts of your business would benefit from deeper, temporary expertise?

- What's the opportunity cost of delay—or of struggling through without support?

Support doesn't have to mean outsourcing strategy. It means reinforcing your team's ability to execute. The smartest leaders are not those who try to carry every load—but those who know when, and how, to ask for help.

In an era defined by speed, change, and increasing complexity, the LIBBi Task Workforce offers one approach to this challenge—demonstrating how businesses can tap into certified, agile talent when and where it's needed most. It's not about replacing your team. It's about making sure your team has the support it needs to lead the transformation.

8. How will you measure and manage growth?

Transformation without direction is chaos. That's why this section prompts you to define clear, achievable goals—typically in 30/60/90-day increments—so you can track your progress, adjust in real time, and build sustainable momentum. You'll also outline how your team will review what's working, identify what needs improvement, and adapt your use of LIBBi as your business evolves.

Think of this as your operational dashboard for change—a living map of progress, learning, and iteration.

Why this matters:

As we explored in Chapter 11, every successful AI transformation depends on two things: clarity and agility. Without measurable goals, it's easy to lose focus—or worse, to misinterpret progress. AI Tasks can generate speed, but you still need to know where you're going and how you'll know when you've arrived.

This section of the playbook is about ensuring that your rollout has checkpoints, not just ambition.

Consider the example of Sweetgreen, the fast-casual restaurant chain that has become known for its use of technology to enhance both customer experience and operational efficiency. When Sweetgreen introduced its digital kitchen strategy—combining AI, mobile ordering, customer personalization, and automated fulfillment—they didn't try to scale all at once. Instead, they set clear 30/60/90-day goals for each new market. They monitored delivery times, app engagement, order customization rates, and employee training milestones. Based on those insights, they tweaked both their technology and their in-store operations—scaling intelligently instead of reactively.

The result? Higher throughput, faster service, stronger customer loyalty, and a model that can flex with changing demand—all without sacrificing culture or product quality.

Use this section to set your own benchmarks:

• What outcomes do you want to achieve in 30 days?

• What capabilities or workflows should be online in 60 days?

• What strategic milestones should be met by 90 days?

Then ask: How will we learn from each step? And how will we adjust accordingly?

Because growth isn't something you measure once—it's something you manage, on purpose, in motion, and with intelligence.

9. What new Tasks would accelerate your business?

This final section invites you to look beyond what's available today and puts you in the position of creating AI for tomorrow. As you assess your workflows, stakeholder needs, and industry challenges, consider where a custom AI Task—tailored to your exact process—could unlock a new level of performance, automation, or customer engagement.

This is your opportunity to identify the gaps—whether it's a task you've never seen before, a workflow unique to your niche, or a system you've always wanted to automate but couldn't find a tool that fit.

Why this matters:

Solutions like LIBBi aren't just libraries of pre-built tools. Done right, an Intelligent Business Management Platform™ solution is an engine for intelligent business design—one that evolves with your business, not in spite of it. If a Task doesn't exist yet, you don't have to wait.

This gives you something few businesses ever have: the ability to co-create your systems, not just consume them.

And in an era where differentiation matters more than ever, that ability is powerful. The businesses that lead will be the ones who don't just use the tools available—they help define the ones that come next.

So ask yourself:

• Where in your operation do you still rely on manual effort or inconsistent processes?

• Where do your team or customers experience delays or confusion?

• What would be the one Task that, if automated, would change everything?

These nine questions weren't designed to slow you down—they were designed to help you move forward with confidence. By walking through your workflows, your data, your stakeholders, and your strategy, you've created a living blueprint for intelligent transformation. One that aligns your values with your vision. One that matches your ambition with a real operational plan.

At its core, this checklist isn't about technology. It's about leadership—your leadership. It's about asking the questions that matter before they become problems. It's about surfacing opportunities before they're lost to hesitation. And most of all, it's about owning the path forward, with a clear head and a strong hand.

So whether you've completed every section or simply used this as a thinking tool, the next step is simple: act. Build momentum. Make the move to AI.

Because in the era of AI for business, the best advantage isn't having all the answers—it's having the courage to ask the right questions, and the clarity to act on them. And now, you have both.

Final Thoughts: Turning Plans into Progress

The roadmap is now in your hands.

You've asked the right questions. You've explored what transformation could—and should—look like in your business. From defining workflows to assessing your data, from reimagining your customer experience to evaluating outdated policies, you now hold something far more powerful than theory.

You hold a playbook for action.

Now, imagine this:

Ellis & Rowe, a 12-person architecture and design firm based in Charleston, had grown steadily for a decade—but growth had come at a cost. Projects were buried in email threads. Vendor coordination relied on repeated phone calls. Billing delays led to missed opportunities. Clients appreciated the design work, but breakdowns in delivery and communication were holding the business back.

Then the partners read this chapter. They took the playbook seriously.

They scored their workflows—by difficulty and strategic importance. They listed every piece of software they used and uncovered more than $3,500 in overlapping monthly spend. They reviewed policies they hadn't touched in years. And most importantly, they identified the people in their business ready to lead change.

One week later, they had already launched three small automation pilots. Two weeks later, they'd streamlined intake and reduced friction in their billing process. By 30 days, their team reported less stress and more clarity. By 60 days, customer response times were faster. By 90 days, they had reduced software costs, improved visibility, and created a foundation for long-term efficiency.

They didn't bring in consultants. They didn't overthink it. They followed a process.

They made the move to AI—one decision at a time.

Now it's your turn.

As this chapter has shown, you don't need to wait for a perfect plan. You don't need to master everything. You just need a place to start—and a willingness to lead.

Whether you complete every section of the playbook or use it simply to guide your thinking, what matters is momentum. *Strategy becomes transformation when it's backed by motion.*

But even the best systems only go so far.

In the next chapter, we return to what matters most: people. Because tools may power the transition, but it's people—your people—who carry it forward. Chapter 12 brings us back to the core of this book: leadership. Not theoretical leadership, but the kind that communicates through uncertainty, empowers through clarity, and earns trust one decision at a time.

In the era of AI for business, leadership isn't optional. It's the difference between disruption—and real transformation.

Chapter 12: Leadership Revisited — Change

While writing Chapter 1 of this book—the one focused on leadership—we had the opportunity to pick the brain of a long-time friend, mentor, investor, and leadership consultant: Tom Hutton. Along with an executive career at IBM, Tom and his business partner built a highly successful chain of Domino's franchises, eventually allowing him to semi-retire and pursue his real passion—helping people become more effective leaders. More specifically, helping them understand their "social style" and how it significantly affects their ability to bring out the best in others.

During our session, I asked Tom what advice he had for us as we set out to write this book. It took him all of three seconds to respond:

> "Start with people and end with people. They're the most important part of any business."

Tom was exactly right.

And as we now enter the age of AI for business, we shouldn't forget this foundational truth: it is still us humans—our teams, our colleagues, and those who look to us for leadership—who remain the most essential element of every successful business. Technology may scale decisions, streamline operations, and generate insights. But leadership begins and ends with people.

So here, at the close of this book, we return to that truth.

As we revisit the subject of leadership in this final chapter, we find ourselves not concluding a narrative, but opening a new one. What began as a reflection on values, vision, and culture now becomes a call to action: to lead not just with conviction, but through change. We offer the concept of change as a fourth action taken by world-class leaders and offer thirteen keys to becoming a master at change management.

In a time when the pace of innovation is exponential—and where uncertainty has become a feature, not a bug—the role of a leader is not to resist change. It is to harness it. AI is reshaping business at every level, as we now all understand. New tools appear weekly. Competitors emerge from unexpected places. Business models evolve faster than talent strategies can adapt.

As a result, leadership must be redefined not as a static trait but as a dynamic, adaptive discipline. In the words of John Kotter, *"Leaders don't just accept change; they create it, accelerate it, and shape it."*

This chapter explores what it means to lead through change. We revisit foundational ideas from earlier chapters, draw on real-world successes and failures, and frame change management not as a side job, but as one of the most essential—and enduring—actions a leader can take.

Because in the end, we started with people. And it's only fitting that we end there too.

Guiding Organizations Through Disruption and Reinvention

Something big just happened.

Did the FBI just show up to seize our servers? Did aliens land? Did our competitor just buy us out overnight? Or maybe it was something subtler but no less seismic—we all showed up on Monday, and everything felt different.

Change had arrived.

This is what it feels like in moments of disruption. It's not always a press release or a board vote. Sometimes it's a new regulation, a sudden dip in performance, a game-changing AI tool, or a shift in customer expectations that renders your model obsolete. Whatever the catalyst, the result is the same: the world you were operating in last week is gone.

To the topic of our book, AI is here. Not looming. Not in beta. It's here—remaking everything from workflows to workforce models. And it's forcing businesses to confront change not as an optional project, but as a condition of survival. It is forcing each of us, as individuals, to change.

In Chapter 1, we explored values-based leadership as the foundation for organizations that endure. But when the environment shifts, those values must do more than offer comfort—they must guide transformation. They become the compass for how we change, not just what we protect. This is our first vital point about leading in a time of change – that our values serve as a compass, when we need one the most.

Take, for example, Home Depot, one of the most recognized names in American retail. Long celebrated for its scale and operational consistency, the company found itself facing new kinds of pressure over the last decade—particularly from digital-first competitors, rising customer expectations around omnichannel shopping, and the logistical bar set by Amazon.

In response, Home Depot didn't just adapt—it transformed, and that transformation spanned both leadership generations and strategic layers.

Craig Menear, who served as CEO from 2014 to 2022, initiated the company's aggressive modernization plan, committing over $11 billion to a long-term transformation strategy known internally as "One Home Depot."

The goal wasn't simply to digitize the customer experience—it was to rebuild the business model from the inside out. Menear's team unified online and in-store systems, overhauled supply chain infrastructure, and empowered associates with mobile tools and real-time inventory access. The company adopted machine learning for product recommendations and scaled delivery options to meet new consumer standards.

But this transformation wasn't solely technological. It was cultural. Menear emphasized that success depended on employee empowerment, customer centricity, and long-term vision—principles deeply aligned with the values-based leadership framework explored in Chapter 1.

When Ted Decker, a veteran Home Depot executive, took over as CEO in 2022 (and later as Chairman), he didn't hit pause—he pressed forward. Decker, who had previously led merchandising and store operations, understood that the transformation required discipline, clarity, and a continued focus on human connection. Under his leadership, Home Depot deepened its commitment to being not just a retailer, but a services provider—an end-to-end platform for homeowners and professionals alike. Evolving, without abandoning their core values.

What makes this transformation even more remarkable is that its foundation was laid decades earlier by Ken Langone, one of Home Depot's co-founders and long-time chairman. Langone helped embed a philosophy that placed trust in frontline employees, clarity in execution, and relentless attention to customer service. His belief in empowering "orange-blooded" associates built a culture that would ultimately make Menear and Decker's transformation possible. Langone famously said, *"You treat the associates with respect, and they'll take care of the customers."*

This continuity of values—from Langone's founding ethos to Menear's transformation to Decker's executional leadership—illustrates the full arc of leadership through change.

Home Depot didn't merely digitize processes. It redefined what it means to serve in a technology-driven, service-intensive economy. It became a model for companies seeking to scale innovation without losing culture, and for leaders who want to navigate volatility without abandoning their foundational principles.

The result? Not just financial outperformance, but an enduring company that evolves without losing its soul.

Now compare that to Blockbuster, which famously had the opportunity to acquire Netflix in its early years and declined. What followed was not just a missed opportunity—it was a textbook case of failed leadership through change.

At its peak, Blockbuster had over 9,000 locations and nearly 60,000 employees. It was not just dominant—it was beloved. Families made "Blockbuster nights" a cultural ritual. But as the market began shifting toward digital delivery, streaming, and personalized subscriptions, Blockbuster's leadership doubled down on the very things that had once made it successful: brick-and-mortar stores, late fee revenue, and in-store upsells.

The leadership team saw Netflix as a niche novelty rather than a disruptive force. Despite multiple internal warnings and strategic proposals that flagged digital as the future, Blockbuster's executive team, under then-CEO John Antioco, initially ignored or deprioritized innovation. In 2000, Netflix offered to sell to Blockbuster for $50 million. The offer was dismissed—

reportedly laughed off. At the time, Blockbuster was generating billions in revenue. What could possibly go wrong?

A lot, it turns out.

When Blockbuster did finally respond, its pivot to streaming came too late, too shallow, and too misaligned with consumer expectations. It launched a service called "Total Access," which initially gained traction, but internal politics and a lack of long-term commitment to digital innovation caused the initiative to stall. Leadership turnover added to the chaos, as the vision shifted without consistency or conviction or alignment with values. Decisions were reactive, not proactive. There was no guiding coalition, no cultural shift, and no real transformation strategy—only a defensive posture aimed at preserving the past.

This is the essential difference between companies that lead through disruption and those that are undone by it. Blockbuster had brand loyalty, capital, and market dominance. What it lacked was leadership willing to confront the future with honesty, urgency, and adaptive strategy.

The lesson is clear, and frames our second key learning about change: it isn't a threat—it's a test. And leadership is how you pass it.

It is worth taking a moment to introduce and discuss John Kotter's landmark framework in "Leading Change"—arguably the most influential change leadership model of the last three decades. Kotter's work is something of a roadmap of how a values-based leader can navigate change. Kotter identifies eight essential steps to lead transformation, paraphrased here and comprising our next eight insights about leading change.

1. Create a Sense of Urgency: Without urgency, there is no momentum. Home Depot's leadership team, under Craig Menear, openly acknowledged the need to modernize both customer experience and back-end operations. They didn't wait for declining revenue—they acted before the cracks became chasms. Blockbuster, on the other hand, dismissed urgency. Despite market shifts and warnings from within, its leaders failed to recognize the existential threat of streaming—and waited until it was too late.

2. Build a Guiding Coalition: Change cannot be led in isolation. Menear didn't delegate the transformation to a side team—he brought in leaders like Ted Decker to co-create the strategy and execution. This group shared conviction, authority, and trust. In contrast, Blockbuster's leadership remained insulated. They failed to assemble a forward-thinking coalition, choosing instead to preserve legacy power structures and ignore internal dissent.

3. Form a Strategic Vision and Initiatives: Kotter emphasizes the importance of clarity: people must understand what is changing and why. Home Depot's "One Home Depot" initiative provided a clear, customer-centric roadmap for integrating physical and digital operations. It wasn't a slogan—it was a mission. Blockbuster lacked a coherent vision. Its late-stage attempt at digital pivoting was unfocused, inconsistent, and failed to resonate with employees or customers.

4. Enlist a Volunteer Army: Buy-in doesn't happen through mandate—it spreads through belief. Home Depot didn't push change onto its workforce—it invited store associates into the process, equipping them with tools and training to participate in the transformation. Blockbuster failed to build belief. Its workforce was left in the dark, demoralized, and disengaged. There was no internal rallying cry—only reactive moves and confusion. You

may, also, recall the question in your *Make the Move to AI* playbook about who will be your army in making the change.

5. Enable Action by Removing Barriers: Bureaucracy kills change. Home Depot broke down internal silos between operations and IT, replaced legacy systems, and empowered employees to suggest improvements and challenge outdated processes. Blockbuster, conversely, was mired in organizational inertia. Decision-making was slow. Innovation initiatives were underfunded. Structural resistance strangled momentum.

6. Generate Short-Term Wins: People need visible proof that progress is happening. Home Depot celebrated milestones—like faster checkouts, improved delivery, and more accurate inventory systems—creating a flywheel of belief. Blockbuster's brief attempt at launching "Total Access" was not only poorly communicated, but lacked follow-through and reinforcement, quickly losing momentum.

7. Sustain Acceleration: One win is not transformation. Home Depot kept pressing: expanding its digital capabilities, deepening its B2B offerings, and modernizing logistics. The transformation endured beyond Menear's tenure under Decker's leadership. Blockbuster declared a pivot but failed to invest in it. Leadership turnover, lack of alignment, and strategic inconsistency stalled any chance at sustained innovation.

8. Institute Change: True transformation is cultural. At Home Depot, innovation, operational agility, and customer obsession are now embedded in how teams work and how decisions are made. The "One Home Depot" vision has become the company's identity. At Blockbuster, no cultural transformation ever took hold. Change wasn't embedded—it was bolted on, half-hearted, and eventually abandoned.

What Kotter's model illustrates—and what history confirms—is that change is a discipline, not a guess. It's not about gut feel or overnight pivots. It's about orchestrated, values-driven action.

For business leaders navigating AI, shifting markets, or internal transformation, the takeaway is clear: disruption is inevitable—but failure is not. The real dividing line between companies that thrive and those that collapse is leadership. Not just leadership in title, but leadership in mindset—the willingness to acknowledge that the landscape has changed and the humility to admit that what got you here may no longer be enough to take you forward.

Change is not the enemy. Even when it's disruptive, even when it arrives faster than expected, change is not a threat to be managed—it's an opportunity to be led. Especially in the age of AI for business, change can be breathtaking. It unlocks entirely new models of productivity, service, and collaboration. It redefines how value is created, and who gets to create it. It's exciting. It's transformational. And it's yours to shape.

What separates enduring organizations from those that vanish is not access to capital or code—it's leadership. The kind of leadership that doesn't wait for certainty but creates clarity in motion. That builds urgency without fear. That treats values not as branding, but as a compass.

Embracing Volatility as a Driver of Innovation

We turn our attention now to the intentional and proactive use of change as a leadership tool—to not just endure volatility, but to leverage it. This is the heart of our eleventh key learning. Volatility, once feared as a source of chaos and instability, is now a signal—one that leaders must learn to read and respond to. In the era of AI, volatility is no longer the enemy of progress—it's the fuel for it. The role of a modern leader is no longer to avoid disruption, but to transform it into momentum.

As AI is introduced into business, resulting in clear change, implementing an Intelligent Business Management Platform™ solution is a great example of bringing transformation out of uncertainty. For example, as we explored in Chapter 9, the evolution from repetitive business tasks to thoughtful AI Task orchestration through LIBBi transforms the routine and repetitive. The space created allows leaders to focus on strategic design, continuous experimentation, and cultural reinvention. It is in this space—where uncertainty meets possibility—that volatility becomes not a threat, but an extraordinary advantage.

Take, for example, a mid-sized general contracting firm based in the Southeast U.S. For decades, the company had operated on trusted instincts, clipboards, whiteboards, and weekly stand-ups. Its reputation was built on reliability, craftsmanship, and long-standing client relationships. But as supply chain disruptions, rising material costs, and labor shortages created volatility across the construction industry, leadership began to feel the pressure. Clients expected faster timelines. Subcontractors needed tighter coordination. Compliance requirements were increasing. And the old systems—manual scheduling, siloed spreadsheets, delayed reporting—were breaking down.

Rather than reacting with cost-cutting or pushing harder on outdated systems, the company's leadership made a bold decision: to treat disruption as a trigger for innovation.

They implemented LIBBi as an Intelligent Business Management Platform™ solution to modernize every aspect of their operations. Project management became orchestrated through Tasks. Scheduling synced across teams and subs. Compliance Tasks auto-triggered document uploads and field reports. Budget insights updated daily through connected data layers. Within weeks, their teams weren't just moving faster—they were making better decisions in real time.

Most importantly, the leadership reframed what change meant. They didn't just digitize paperwork—they empowered field managers to suggest process improvements, gave office staff better tools, and brought clients into the loop with real-time dashboards. The firm didn't lose its personal touch—it amplified it.

This story reflects what John Kotter and Vanessa Akhtar describe in *Change: How Organizations Achieve Hard-to-Imagine Results in Uncertain Times*. They emphasize that modern leaders must live in duality—retaining the stability of traditional structures while activating agile, empowered networks. This general contractor did just that: preserving its culture of craftsmanship while evolving into a more connected, data-driven, AI-supported business.

Now consider a very different industry: a regional accounting firm serving small businesses and nonprofits. Historically, their model was built around seasonal peaks—tax filings, quarterly closes, and year-end audits. But over time, client expectations shifted. They wanted year-round insights, faster reporting, and proactive financial advice. Automation tools like QuickBooks, Xero, and AI-based tax bots were reducing the need for routine input services. Many accounting firms saw this trend and panicked—cutting staff, shrinking scope, or doubling down on compliance-only offerings.

But this firm took a different route. They leaned into the change.

They used LIBBi to orchestrate client onboarding, automate document collection, and create AI Tasks that delivered rolling cash flow insights, financial benchmarks, and compliance alerts. Staff time was reallocated from paperwork to partnership. They even created a new client portal powered by LIBBi by simply subscribing to that Task, allowing business owners to ask questions, generate reports, and launch tasks with natural language prompts.

Rather than fear automation, the firm redefined its value around interpretation and guidance. And clients responded—with higher retention, more referrals, and expanded service requests.

What made this shift work wasn't just the technology. It was leadership willing to embrace volatility as a chance to get better, not smaller.

You are now very familiar with *The Leadership Challenge* by James Kouzes and Barry Posner, which describes five practices of exemplary leadership that guide teams through uncertain times. One of those practices—Challenge the Process—calls on leaders to step outside routine, question assumptions, and look for smarter ways to operate. The businesses above did exactly that. They didn't wait for the pressure to ease. They used it as fuel.

What's more, their leaders also embodied Enable Others to Act—another principle in the Kouzes and Posner framework. By trusting team members to engage, contribute, and shape the transition, they built commitment, not just compliance.

It is worth noting that the right solution makes this kind of responsive leadership tangible. A modular structure allows for iterative innovation—one Task at a time. Leaders can try, test, learn, and scale without committing to multi-year, high-risk implementations. The right platform becomes a living lab for frontline experimentation and strategic agility.

Volatility will continue. Market demands will shift. But businesses that treat disruption as design input—rather than as a threat—will stay ahead. They'll build cultures of experimentation, agility, and shared ownership.

And those cultures don't start with dashboards or policies. They start with leaders willing to change before the market forces them to—leaders who see volatility not as a breakdown, but as a doorway.

Because in an AI-driven world, adaptability isn't just a skill—it's the advantage.

Communicating Stability While Encouraging Transformation

Leadership is not only about setting direction—it's about creating environments of trust. Especially in times of uncertainty, trust becomes the emotional infrastructure on which progress depends.

As Brené Brown writes in *Dare to Lead*, "Clear is kind. Unclear is unkind." In times of transformation, resistance often stems from the anxiety of disconnection—of being untethered from what's familiar, rather fear of the unknown. The solution is leadership grounded in clarity and trust— leadership that honors where people have been while guiding them toward where they need to go. The skill lies in communicating, *"We are evolving,"* without making people feel like, *"We're leaving everything behind."*

This is leadership as an art form. It's, also, our twelfth key teaching on leading change.

The best leaders are those who understand that change doesn't land well when it feels like abandonment. It lands when it feels like growth with a guide. Great leaders know how to create psychological safety while introducing strategic risk. They offer a clear narrative: where we're going, why it matters, and what's staying constant. This narrative doesn't sugarcoat the journey—it gives people a reason to stay committed through it.

This teaching was deeply present in our early discussions about creating our core product. We both had experienced multiple periods of change in our business environments, most recently the impact of COVID-19 in the workplace. While we were both leading completely different organizations at the time, we, like so many others, faced the exact same challenge and opportunity to change in a way we desired. Disruption had arrived, no one knew how long it would last, change was required, and moving to a remote and virtual workforce was the right solution for our businesses. We both found different but powerful technology that made this change more manageable, although not perfect. I recall our discussion about what it would have been like to have a solution like the LIBBi we imagined during the disruption of COVID-19. The ability for our company to rapidly identify the new necessities like a high-functioning video conference solution, real-time document collaboration, and a travel coordinating system that considered local restrictions – for amazing developers to create these in rapid order – and for businesses to implement with a single click. Further, for employees to use the Tasks with ease, borrowing strongly from the intuitive and simple chat-based interface. Wow, we thought. Ultimately, success in this element of leading change is about communicating the transformation with clarity and credibility. And, if its LIBBi or another powerful tool, using technology to enhance your communication as a leader is vital in this age of AI for business. Some process examples:

- When Task performance is visible in real-time, employees feel like participants—not bystanders.

- When system evolution is documented and accessible, fear of the unknown gives way to informed curiosity.

- When workforce development is trackable, teams see themselves growing with the business—not being left behind.

This visibility turns abstract "change" into measurable progress, creating the kind of narrative that builds momentum and mitigates fear.

As we shared in Chapter 10, one of the keys to successful adoption is making learning continuous and visible. People feel safer when they know the system is tracking development—not judging it. When they can see where the business is headed—and where they fit in that journey—they are far more likely to engage.

Leaders can't control every outcome, but they can control the tone and transparency with which change is introduced. They can reinforce values even while evolving processes. They can honor legacy even as they pursue transformation.

In this way, transformation doesn't destabilize—it re-grounds. It gives people a new framework for growth, purpose, and contribution. When that happens, resistance fades, and change becomes not a loss, but a shared achievement.

And that, ultimately, is the job of the modern leader: not to push change onto their teams, but to walk them through it—anchored, informed, and inspired.

Developing Change-Resilient Leaders and Teams

Values-based leadership is not just personal—it's cultural. And nowhere is that more vital than in how organizations develop resilience, our change management hack number thirteen. In times of transformation, businesses must do more than implement new tools—they must foster the mindset, habits, and human systems that make adaptation sustainable.

We saw this vividly in Chapter 10 with IBM's *SkillsBuild* program. IBM didn't just reskill for technical capacity—it created a culture of continuous reinvention, making learning core to the employee experience. While IBM is a large enterprise, the same principles apply—and may be even more urgent—for small and mid-sized businesses, where talent is often lean and every team member plays a critical role.

Take, for example, Fireclay Tile, a California-based artisan tile manufacturer. A company rooted in craft and tradition, Fireclay faced a moment of truth in the early 2010s. The real estate downturn had slowed demand, and cheaper overseas competitors were cutting into the market. Rather than resort to layoffs or deep cost-cutting, CEO Eric Edelson made a bold choice: to double down on people and culture.

He flattened hierarchies, implemented open-book management, and invested in design, operations, and digital marketing training for his team. He moved the business toward a made-to-order model and gave employees access to new tools and customer engagement platforms. As a result, Fireclay became not just more efficient—but more innovative. Its culture shifted from "handcrafted but fragile" to "artisanal and adaptable." Today, Fireclay is thriving, having expanded its workforce, customer base, and reputation—all by putting learning and change at the center of its values.

Now consider Union Kitchen, a Washington D.C.-based food incubator and small business accelerator. Union Kitchen's model is built around supporting early-stage food startups, offering everything from commercial kitchen space to marketing help. But during the COVID-19 pandemic, many of its startup partners saw their retail pipelines collapse. Rather than retreat, Union Kitchen's leadership pivoted fast—introducing e-commerce training, updating packaging workflows, and launching centralized delivery networks to help member businesses survive.

The leadership didn't just react to disruption—they empowered their community to rethink and rebuild. That investment paid off. Dozens of Union Kitchen graduates not only stayed in business—they grew, proving that resilient teams aren't built in calm—they're forged in uncertainty.

This stands in sharp contrast to what happened with Circuit City, once a major electronics retailer. In a now-infamous move, the company laid off its most experienced salespeople in an effort to trim costs. The result was catastrophic: customer service collapsed, morale eroded, and innovation stopped. Rather than nurturing its change agents, Circuit City eliminated them—and soon after, the business collapsed entirely.

This is where Adam Grant's *Think Again* offers a powerful insight: in a world of constant transformation, success depends less on what we know and more on how quickly we can unlearn and relearn. The best leaders don't just pass knowledge down—they build systems that reward curiosity, humility, and growth. They create a systematic approach to resilience.

Leaders who create a culture of resilience ensure that their businesses don't just survive change—they build the muscle memory to lead through it. They create workplaces where innovation is decentralized, where learning is ongoing, and where every disruption becomes a new opportunity to grow.

In the end, resilience is not about bracing for impact—it's about becoming the kind of leader and team that runs toward change, not away from it.

Final Thoughts

Throughout this book, we have returned to the timeless principles of leadership—vision, culture, values, endurance, and now change. In Chapter 1, we began with the foundational truth that leadership is not just what you do—it's who you choose to be. In this final chapter, we reaffirm that leadership is also a discipline of adaptive stability: the ability to embrace change without abandoning purpose, to evolve without eroding identity.

The pace of transformation—technological, economic, and cultural—will only accelerate from here. But as we've seen through the lens of Kotter's eight steps, the insights of Akhtar and Grant, and the real-world stories of businesses that rose or fell during moments of disruption, one truth holds steady: leadership is what turns volatility into progress.

Great business solutions, like LIBBi, give leaders the tools to act decisively—without compromising values. To innovate—without losing the plot. To move fast—but remain grounded in transparency, trust, and clarity. The tools provide the infrastructure, the orchestration, and the learning systems—but it's people who lead.

The organizations that successfully navigate AI for business are the ones who build cultures of curiosity, confidence, and contribution. They are led by those who understand that transformation is an ongoing practice of vision, empathy, and intentional decision-making.

As Kotter reminds us, change leadership is not just about managing projects—it's about managing mindsets. As Adam Grant teaches, resilience comes from being willing to Think Again—to let go of what no longer serves and embrace what might. And as Kouzes and Posner show us, great leaders Challenge the Process, Inspire a Shared Vision, and Enable Others to Act. With the thirteen keys to managing change that we've now discussed, you can be exactly that leader.

The playbook for the future isn't written in code. It's written in courage.

And it's lived by leaders who choose action over inertia. Learning over certainty. And people over process.

We've shown you the tools. We've shared the principles. Now the next move belongs to you.

The future isn't waiting.

And leadership—your leadership—is how we meet it. It is, we know, all about people.

Conclusion: Building What Comes Next

We began this book with a simple, human truth—one that now feels even more urgent, more relevant, and more real:

People build businesses. AI helps us run them better.

Twelve chapters later, we've explored what that means in practice. We've seen how leadership, when grounded in values, becomes the anchor in a sea of technological disruption. We've made the case that artificial intelligence is not just a feature or a trend—it's a force multiplier, capable of scaling what we design, what we believe, and what we lead.

And most importantly, we've shown that this moment is not reserved for Silicon Valley, for research labs, or trillion-dollar companies. It's for you—the business operator. The owner. The builder. The team leader navigating change. The entrepreneur chasing clarity and execution. The person who sees the future and chooses to build toward it instead of waiting for it.

AI is here. And this book has been about giving you the tools, the frameworks, and the language to use it not just intelligently—but intentionally.

Now, at the end of this journey, we circle back to where we started: with you.

The difference is that now, you're not just wondering what AI might mean for your business. You're holding the playbook to shape it.

The next move belongs to you.

What You've Just Learned

Over these twelve chapters, you haven't just explored artificial intelligence—you've explored the anatomy of intelligent business. You've gone from high-level concepts to practical frameworks. You've seen real-world examples, read bold predictions, and encountered timeless truths. But more than anything, you've been given a mirror and a map: a reflection of the leader you are, and a guide to where you're going.

We began in Chapter 1, not with hype, but with humility—by returning to the timeless principles that underpin every enduring business: vision, culture, and endurance. You were reminded that leadership doesn't get automated—it gets amplified. That values are not a backdrop to AI—they are the infrastructure it will scale. That in a time of change, the best leaders are not those who move the fastest, but those who lead with purpose.

In Chapter 2, we talked ethics—not as a footnote, but as a feature. We explored the frameworks and global efforts to create safe, transparent, and accountable AI systems. You learned that ethics is not a compliance checklist—it's a design principle. And that in the world of AI, your values show up in your algorithms.

Then we stepped back to look forward. Chapters 3 through 5 gave you the lay of the land: the philosophical roots and technical foundations of AI, the real business applications transforming companies today, and the waves of convergence, decentralization, and intelligent marketplaces that are reshaping what tomorrow will look like.

As we said in Chapter 3: *"You can't lead where you don't understand."* Now you understand. And now, you can lead.

But understanding isn't enough. So in Chapter 6, we helped you clear the fog. We cut through the buzzwords, the startup promises, the endless tools—and asked a better question: What actually works for your business?

That led us to Chapter 7, where the future came into focus. You were introduced to AI Tasks—modular, intelligent, orchestrated actions that bring automation to life. We moved from the abstract to the actionable. From theory to toolset. You saw how intelligent workflows could be launched, scaled, and aligned with real business outcomes. This was the moment AI became real.

Then we came back to what's always been at the heart of business: people.

Chapters 8 through 10 made it clear: your workforce isn't being replaced—it's being reimagined. You learned how to structure your data so it fuels intelligent operations rather than obstructing them. You discovered how to shift your team from execution to orchestration—from managing chaos to leading systems. You saw how AI can elevate every role—from technician to strategist—and how LIBBi supports a workforce model built on learning, collaboration, and agility.

We introduced you to new roles: Task Generalists, who activate value across functions. Task Specialists, who deepen impact in specific domains. We helped you see how to certify, support, and scale your team—without adding unnecessary complexity or overhead.

Then came the moment of action.

In Chapter 11, you were given the Make the Move to AI Playbook—nine questions designed to transform ideas into intelligent movement. You evaluated your workflows, your systems, your stakeholders, your platforms, and your policies. You built—or began to build—a roadmap for transformation. And you met companies like Ellis & Rowe, who didn't wait for the perfect moment. They made the move. They acted. They learned. They grew.

Finally, in Chapter 12, we returned to where it all began: leadership. But this time, in motion. In the face of change. You identified thirteen keys to change. You reflected on stories of businesses that embraced volatility and others that clung to the past. You were reminded that change doesn't just test systems—it tests people. And that while AI may be scaling everything, it's leadership that determines what actually gets scaled.

Throughout this book, one message has remained consistent:

You don't need to be a technologist to lead in the age of AI. You just need the clarity to ask the right questions—and the courage to act on them.

That's what you've just learned.

And now, you're ready to navigate AI for your business.

What Comes Next

So, what now?

Maybe you've filled out the checklist. Maybe you've already launched your first Task. Maybe you're still thinking, still evaluating, still standing on the edge of transformation.

Wherever you are—this book has one last message for you:

Just start.

History rarely gives us perfect conditions for bold moves. The leaders who shaped turning points didn't wait for a full plan. They moved when they had a window—and made the plan along the way.

In 1961, when President Kennedy committed to landing a man on the moon by the end of the decade, the United States had only achieved 15 minutes of human spaceflight. There was no roadmap. The rocket didn't exist. The technology hadn't been invented. But the direction was clear. Kennedy didn't ask for guarantees—he asked for movement. And that momentum gave rise to one of the greatest innovations in human history.

You're standing in a similar moment in business transformation. AI has opened a frontier. And the question is no longer *"Will it matter?"* The question is:

Who will you choose to be in this moment? A question borrowed from one of my mentors, Greg Harbaugh, who perhaps was asked the same by those who challenged him.

Will you be the business that waits for certainty? Or the one that acts with purpose?

Will you be the leader who hesitates until everything's mapped—or the one who understands that clarity comes through movement, not before it?

You don't need to master everything. You just need to move something. One Task. One process. One conversation with your team. That's where momentum begins. That's where learning starts. That's where change becomes reality.

You now have the frameworks. The language. What matters most is how you lead, what you build, and who you bring with you.

Because the future won't belong to the businesses with the most tools.

It will belong to the ones who had the courage to start.

The vision to adapt.

And the leadership to keep going.

A Final Word

This era of AI for business is about people who are willing to reimagine what's possible—willing to use intelligence, both human and artificial, to build systems that reflect their values and serve their communities.

This is your moment.

Real people. Solving real problems. Running real businesses.

So take the lead. Navigate with clarity. Build with conviction.

And let's make the move to intelligent business—together.

Now, go build what comes next.

References:

Chapter 1: The Timeless Core — Why Leadership Still Matters

Bezos, J., & The Long Now Foundation. (n.d.). Long-term thinking and corporate responsibility. Retrieved from https://longnow.org

Cadbury, G. (n.d.). Leadership actions and the Bournville model. Derived from historical records and CSR studies in industrial England.

Chernow, R. (1998). *Titan: The life of John D. Rockefeller, Sr.* Random House. *Includes detail on Standard Oil's growth, antitrust intervention, and Rockefeller's later philanthropic evolution.*

Collins, J. (2009). *How the mighty fall: And why some companies never give in.* HarperBusiness.
Also mentioned in articles from Harvard Business Review and Bloomberg.

Gallo, C. (2014). *The Apple experience: Secrets to building insanely great customer loyalty.* McGraw-Hill.

George, B. (2003). *Authentic leadership: Rediscovering the secrets to creating lasting value.* Jossey-Bass.

Grant, A. (2021). *Think again: The power of knowing what you don't know.* Viking.

Holy Bible, Luke 12:48 (New International Version or translation of choice)

Isaacson, W. (2023). *Elon Musk.* Simon & Schuster.

Johnson, R. D. (2006). *Global business leadership.* DaVinci Press.

Joly, H. (2021). *The heart of business: Leadership principles for the next era of capitalism.* Harvard Business Review Press.

Kouzes, J. M., & Posner, B. Z. (2017). *The leadership challenge: How to make extraordinary things happen in organizations* (6th ed.). Wiley.

Langone, K. (2018). *I love capitalism!: An American story.* Portfolio.

Mandela, N. (1994). *Long walk to freedom: The autobiography of Nelson Mandela.* Little, Brown and Company.

Maxwell, J. C. (2007). *The 21 irrefutable laws of leadership: Follow them and people will follow you.* Thomas Nelson.

McLean, B., & Elkind, P. (2003). *The smartest guys in the room: The amazing rise and scandalous fall of Enron.* Portfolio.

Polman, P. (2009–2018). Unilever leadership initiatives. Referenced via public company reports and interviews.

Sinek, S. (2018). *The Navy SEAL performance vs. trust matrix* [Video]. U.S. Navy Special Operations leadership interviews. Retrieved from https://www.youtube.com/watch?v=RyTQ5-SQYTo

Chapter 2: The Ethical Compass — Ethics and Guardrails for the Age of AI

Coeckelbergh, M. (2020). *AI ethics.* MIT Press.

Davis, K. (2012). *Ethics of big data: Balancing risk and innovation.* O'Reilly Media.

European Commission. (2021). *Proposal for a regulation laying down harmonised rules on artificial intelligence (Artificial Intelligence Act).*

Jobin, A., Ienca, M., & Vayena, E. (2019). *The global landscape of AI ethics guidelines.* Nature Machine Intelligence, 1(9), 389–399.

Kotter, J. P., & Akhtar, V. (2021). *Change: How organizations achieve hard-to-imagine results in uncertain times.* Wiley.

National Institute of Standards and Technology (NIST). (2023). *AI risk management framework (AI RMF 1.0).*

OECD. (2019). *OECD principles on artificial intelligence.*

OpenAI. (2018). *OpenAI Charter.* Retrieved from https://openai.com/charter

Schmidt, E., Kissinger, H. A., & Huttenlocher, D. (2021). *The age of AI: And our human future*. Little, Brown and Company.

UNESCO. (2021). *Recommendation on the ethics of artificial intelligence*.

Wallach, W., & Allen, C. (2008). *Moral machines: Teaching robots right from wrong*. Oxford University Press.

Chapter 3: The Path to Now — A Brief History of AI

Anderson, J. L. (2021). *Artificial intelligence for business: A roadmap for profitable and responsible AI adoption*. Future Insights Publishing.

Brown, T. B., et al. (2020). Language models are few-shot learners. *arXiv preprint* arXiv:2005.14165.

Coeckelbergh, M. (2020). *AI ethics*. MIT Press.

Davis, K. (2012). *Ethics of big data: Balancing risk and innovation*. O'Reilly Media.

European Commission. (2021). *The artificial intelligence act*.

Krizhevsky, A., Sutskever, I., & Hinton, G. E. (2012). ImageNet classification with deep convolutional neural networks. In *Advances in neural information processing systems* (pp. 1097–1105).

Lee, K.-F. (2021). *AI 2041: Ten visions for our future*. Currency.

Lu, Y., et al. (2023). BloombergGPT: A large language model for finance. *arXiv preprint* arXiv:2304.03285.

Minsky, M. (1975). A framework for representing knowledge. In P. H. Winston (Ed.), *The psychology of computer vision* (pp. 211–277). McGraw-Hill.

Minsky, M. (1986). *The society of mind*. Simon & Schuster.

NIST. (2023). *AI risk management framework (AI RMF 1.0)*.

OECD. (2019). *OECD principles on artificial intelligence*.

OpenAI. (2018). *OpenAI Charter.* https://openai.com/charter

OpenAI. (2022). *ChatGPT release notes.* https://openai.com/blog/chatgpt

Rumelhart, D. E., Hinton, G. E., & Williams, R. J. (1986). Learning representations by back-propagating errors. *Nature*, 323, 533–536.

Schmidt, E., Kissinger, H. A., & Huttenlocher, D. (2021). *The age of AI: And our human future.* Little, Brown and Company.

Suleyman, M. (2023). *The coming wave: Technology, power, and the twenty-first century's greatest dilemma.* Crown Publishing.

Turing, A. M. (1950). *Computing machinery and intelligence. Mind*, 59(236), 433–460.

University of Pennsylvania. (1945). *ENIAC project documentation.* Moore School of Electrical Engineering.

UNESCO. (2021). *Recommendation on the ethics of artificial intelligence.*

Von Neumann, J. (1945). *First draft of a report on the EDVAC.* University of Pennsylvania.

Wallach, W., & Allen, C. (2008). *Moral machines: Teaching robots right from wrong.* Oxford University Press.

Chapter 4: The AI Roadmap and Emerging Business Solutions

Anderson, J. L. (2021). *Artificial intelligence for business: A roadmap for profitable and responsible AI adoption.* Future Insights Publishing.

Anthropic. (2023). *Claude model overview.* Retrieved from https://www.anthropic.com

Agrawal, A., Gans, J., & Goldfarb, A. (2018). *Prediction machines: The simple economics of artificial intelligence.* Harvard Business Review Press.

Auto-GPT. (2023). *GitHub repository.* Retrieved from https://github.com/Torantulino/Auto-GPT

CrewAI. (2023). *Agent orchestration framework.* Retrieved from https://github.com/joaomdmoura/crewai

Davis, K. (2012). *Ethics of big data: Balancing risk and innovation.* O'Reilly Media.

European Commission. (2021). *The artificial intelligence act.*

Google DeepMind. (2023). *Gemini technical specifications.* Retrieved from https://deepmind.google/technologies/gemini/

IBM. (1997). *Deep Blue defeats Garry Kasparov.* Retrieved from https://www.ibm.com/ibm/history/ibm100/us/en/icons/deepblue/

Lee, K.-F. (2021). *AI 2041: Ten visions for our future.* Currency.

NIST. (2023). *AI risk management framework (AI RMF 1.0).*

Liu, H., et al. (2023). *LLaVA: Large Language-and-Vision Assistant.* arXiv preprint arXiv:2304.08485.

OECD. (2019). *OECD principles on artificial intelligence.*

Schmidt, E., Kissinger, H. A., & Huttenlocher, D. (2021). *The age of AI: And our human future.* Little, Brown and Company.

OpenAI. (2023). *GPT-4 technical report.* Retrieved from https://openai.com/research/gpt-4

Suleyman, M. (2023). *The coming wave: Technology, power, and the twenty-first century's greatest dilemma.* Crown Publishing.

UNESCO. (2021). *Recommendation on the ethics of artificial intelligence.*

Wallach, W., & Allen, C. (2008). *Moral machines: Teaching robots right from wrong.* Oxford University Press.

Chapter 5: Five Years Forward — The Coming Wave

Gates, B. (1995). *The internet tidal wave.* Microsoft internal memo. Retrieved from https://www.gatesnotes.com

Goldman Sachs. (2023). *The potentially large effects of artificial intelligence on economic growth.* Goldman Sachs Research.

Goertzel, B., & Pennachin, C. (2007). *Artificial General Intelligence.* Springer.

Iansiti, M., & Lakhani, K. R. (2020). *Competing in the age of AI: Strategy and leadership when algorithms and networks run the world.* Harvard Business Review Press.

McKinsey & Company. (2024). *The state of AI in 2024: Generative AI's breakout year.* Retrieved from https://www.mckinsey.com

OpenAI. (2023). *AutoGPT and emerging agentic frameworks.* OpenAI Blog.

OpenAI. (2023). *AutoGPT and emerging agentic frameworks.* OpenAI Blog.

Suleyman, M. (2023). *The coming wave: Technology, power, and the twenty-first century's greatest dilemma.* Crown Publishing.

Torantulino. (2023). *Auto-GPT GitHub repository.* Retrieved from https://github.com/Torantulino/Auto-GPT

U.S. Congress. (2022). *CHIPS and Science Act of 2022.* Public Law No: 117-167. Retrieved from https://www.congress.gov

Wong, L., et al. (2023). *ReAct: Reasoning and Acting in Language Models.* arXiv:2210.03629.

Chapter 6: Cutting Through the Noise and Finding Simplicity

Anthony, S. D. (2016). *Kodak's downfall wasn't about technology.* Harvard Business Review. https://hbr.org/2016/07/kodaks-downfall-wasnt-about-technology

Cagan, M., & Jones, C. (2018). *INSPIRED: How to create tech products customers love.* Wiley.

Gartner. (2023). *AI hype cycle: Market saturation, orchestration, and platform consolidation.* Gartner Research.

Grant, A. (2021). *Think again: The power of knowing what you don't know.* Viking.